THE SONS O

JESUS AND THE

David Gaston

"It is very surprising that the Essenes, whose exemplary virtues elicited the unbounded admiration of even the Greeks and Romans, and whose doctrines and practices contributed so materially to the spread of Christianity, should be so little known about among intelligent Christians."

(Dr Christian Ginsberg, writing in 1869)

CONTENTS

1. Introduction
2. A Day in Jerusalem
3. Josephus and the Essenes
4. Essenes and their Possessions
5. Essenes and their Practices
6. Essenes and Marriage
7. Essenes, Oaths and Anger
8. The Sermon on the Mount
9. Essene Teachings and the Letter of James
10. The Second Temple Period
11. The Magi, King Cyrus and the Zoroastrians
12. The Bible, Angels and Stars
13. Angels and Archangels
14. Demons and Illness
15. Sadducees and Pharisees
16. Essenes, Authority and Roman Coins
17. Qumran Community Life
18. Education, Toilets and the Sabbath
19. Death, Burial and Resurrection
20. Josephus and the Essene Oaths

21. Jesus and the Essenes
22. The Prodigal's Brother
23. The Qumran Leaders and the Unjust Steward
24. The New Temple and the New Jerusalem
25. Baptism, Locusts and Wild Honey
26. The Clearing of the Temple
27. Enoch and the Calendar
28. The Book of 1 Enoch
29. Hey, Jude!
30. 'The Nephilim' and the Spirits in Prison
31. Fallen Angels and 'the Abyss'
32. Jude, 2 Peter and 'Celestial Beings'
33. 1 Enoch and the Book of Revelation
34. 'Son of Man'
35. 'Son of God'
36. Qumran Fragments 4Q246 and 4Q521
37. 'Works of the Law' and 4QMMT
38. Secrets and Ascensions
39. Jannes, Belial and Melchizedek
40. Full Circle

1. INTRODUCTION

"Jesus was an Essene." The presenter's confident assertion astounded me! To be honest, I hadn't been giving the TV documentary my full attention, but now I found myself sitting bolt upright. "WHAT?! Hold on a minute! Can you repeat that?" I wanted to ask. Alas, he had gone on to talk about something else. His matter-of-fact statement had, however, been left firmly imprinted on my mind.

I had never come across any references in my Bible to Essenes. They weren't mentioned in any of the sermons I'd ever heard or in any Christian books I'd read. So, from where, I wondered, did this man get the idea **Jesus** was an Essene?

During a memorable visit to Israel several years earlier, I had learned that the Essenes (pronounced "Ess-eens") were a devout Jewish sect who are thought to have hidden the Dead Sea Scrolls – the amazing ancient documents discovered between 1947 and 1956 inside jars in remote caves in the Judean desert. But that was about all I knew. I resolved to find out more.

Although not mentioned by name in the Bible, the Essenes, I was to discover, were a significant Jewish party (or denomination) at the time of Jesus. We know this from the records of the first century Jewish writer Josephus and those of other ancient historians, who between them have quite a lot to say about the Essenes and their practices. Most experts believe that the group who at one time inhabited the now-excavated ruins in the desert at **Qumran**, about 40 km east of Jerusalem and not far from the Dead Sea, were a community of Essenes and the Dead Sea Scrolls hidden in nearby caves were, in effect, the Essenes' library.

I found the subject of the Essenes to be a fascinating one. Living simply and sharing their food and clothing, they had forsaken personal possessions to pursue righteousness and the kingdom of God.

They believed in an on-going battle between good and evil, in angels and in demons, in eternal punishment for the unrighteous and in eternal life for the elect few.

As I researched the Essenes and their books, it led me (much to my surprise) to Bible passages I'd always found a little obscure or that didn't quite seem to me to fit. There are several such verses in the Bible, which had always left me with the impression there is a good deal more behind what is written than meets the eye.

One example is the statement of Jesus (quoted in Matthew 19:24) that it is easier for a camel to go through the eye of a needle than it is for a **rich** man to enter the kingdom of God. Another is this most unusual passage at the start of Genesis 6, just before the story of Noah and the Flood:

> *When human beings began to increase in number on the earth and daughters were born to them, the sons of God saw that the daughters of humans were beautiful, and they married any of them they chose. Then the Lord said, "My spirit will not contend with humans for ever, for they are mortal. Their days will be 120 years". The Nephilim were on the earth in those days – and afterwards – when the sons of God went to the daughters of humans and had children by them.*

There is an equally puzzling reference in 1 Peter 3:19 to Christ preaching to spirits in prison, who are said to have been disobedient in the days of Noah. Then there is the Apostle Paul's mention in 2 Corinthians 12 of a man's mysterious ascension to *"the third heaven"*. And then, in Luke 16, we have the Parable of the Unjust Steward (or Dishonest Manager) in which the steward was commended for fraudulently using his master's wealth in order to make friends for himself.

In my experience, these Bible passages are seldom referred to by Christian writers or preachers. I now recognise that I, too, had sought to put them out of my mind and concentrate on verses which are more easily understood and applied. As a result of my discoveries, however, these seemingly difficult passages (on which I will be reflecting in this book) have taken on a new significance.

Although I'd heard sermons on the topic of the Transfiguration, I confess I was always left with the feeling that, in relation to this major event in the life of Jesus, I didn't entirely 'get it'. I was similarly perplexed by the reference in Luke 15:7 to *"righteous persons who do not need to repent"* and wondered who the prodigal son's faithful brother in the parable recounted in Luke 15 was intended to represent. I also had a nagging feeling of never having been provided with a truly satisfactory explanation of Jesus' frequent use of the title *"the Son of Man"*.

I was disconcerted by the passing reference in 2 Timothy 3:8 to *"Jannes and Jambres"* (characters who aren't mentioned anywhere else in the Bible) and by another in Jude to the archangel Michael having had some sort of dispute with the Devil about the body of Moses. These references pointed beyond what was contained in my Bible, challenging my assertion that the Old and New Testaments comprise a complete and independent whole. Before commencing my research, however, I had no idea from where they had come.

This book is an attempt to consider some of the Essene's beliefs and relate them to the New Testament. It doesn't seek to expound these Bible passages (something I am woefully unqualified to do) but I trust it will shed some light on them. Many readers will no doubt already be familiar with details of which I was in ignorance. But I hope that others – especially those who, as I was, are unfamiliar with the Essenes – will find it informative.

As someone who is much more interested in facts than in opinions, I am not going to spend a lot of time opinionating. I am conscious that, as a result, you may perhaps feel you are being led rather aimlessly through a series of random facts. If you find my approach seems at times to be lacking in direction, please bear with me and all (hopefully) will eventually fall into place.

There are many writers and preachers (not to mention TV presenters!) who give their opinions as **being** fact – a practice I've tried to avoid. Scholars, on the other hand, write a thesis, putting forward a theory and then presenting evidence in support. Being a lawyer and not a biblical or historical scholar, however, I am acutely aware of the temptation when writing a thesis to concentrate only on the evidence which supports your theory and resolutely ignore all that doesn't!

My approach is a different one and, as I make no claim to be a scholar, this is not intended to be a thesis. I have no grand overall theory I'm attempting to prove and no fixed position I'm seeking to justify. My aim as a simple layman is instead to outline what I've discovered, leaving readers to draw **their own** conclusions. As it isn't a thesis, I've chosen not to clutter the book with long lists of citations but have instead sought to provide sufficient details of my sources to enable readers in this digital information age to check the facts for themselves.

In Chapter 2, I recall the day I first came to hear of *'the Sons of Light'* and reflect on the dual theme of darkness and light, one which was central to Essene thinking.

Chapters 3-9 look at some of the principal beliefs and practices of the Essenes, noting similarities with the teachings of Jesus. Similarity alone does not of course mean there was a direct connection between them, but you may nevertheless find the parallels to be remarkable.

There is a change of tack in Chapter 10, when I try to (very) briefly summarise the history of the period leading up to the birth of Jesus, an era known as 'the late Second Temple Period'.

Then, drawing on a couple of offbeat observations about the Nativity stories, Chapters 11-15 explore some of the popular ideas which were around at the time and how they impacted the three largest Jewish denominations: the Pharisees, the Sadducees and the Essenes. This, I hope, will help to place the Essenes in an historical and theological context.

In Chapters 16-24 we return once more to the subject of the Essenes themselves, looking at some more Essene beliefs and viewing (or reviewing) various passages from the Gospels in the light of these.

Chapter 25 considers the intriguing person we know as John the Baptist. And Chapter 26 reflects upon the decisive occasion (or perhaps occasions) when Jesus forcibly cleared the Temple in Jerusalem.

Chapters 27-33 are about the Book of 1 Enoch, which was a favourite of the Essenes. This curious Book has some interesting connections with the New Testament, and in particular with the Letter of Jude and the Book of Revelation (or 'the Apocalypse').

Chapters 34-36 briefly look at the titles *'the Son of Man'*, *'the Son of God'* and *'the Messiah'* and their use both in the Bible and in the Dead Sea Scrolls (also sometimes referred to as 'the Qumran Scrolls' or simply as 'the Scrolls').

Chapters 37-39 attempt to consider some more Bible passages in the light of the Scrolls. And finally, Chapter 40 comprises a summary and a few concluding comments.

You will no doubt be glad to find that most of the chapters are short, enabling you to take it at your own pace. If you are unfamiliar with the information, I suggest that you take only two or three chapters at a time rather than attempting too many at the one sitting.

Some words in the book have been highlighted for emphasis. In all cases the highlighting has been done by me.

2. A DAY IN JERUSALEM

There are days in life which live on in the memory, coming back to mind time and again, providing inspiration. One such day for me took place in the historic city of Jerusalem, during the visit to Israel I mentioned in the previous Chapter.

I had really been looking forward to the trip. As an evangelical Christian brought up in a Plymouth Brethren family with a strong sense of faith and identity, I had come to love the person of Jesus Christ portrayed in the New Testament, the Son of God who left the glory of heaven and came to earth to give His life for sinners like me. I was keen to experience for myself something of the land in which Jesus had lived.

On the day in question, my wife and I first visited *Yad Vashem*, the Holocaust World Remembrance Centre. It is somewhere we will long remember, not least the poignant memorial to the one-and-a-half million Jewish children whose lives were so cruelly cut short in the horrific evil of the Holocaust. Inside this building thousands of tiny candles shine out in the sombre darkness like the countless stars of the night sky, the beautiful 'host of heaven'. It was a truly moving experience.

I find it deeply disturbing that some who profess allegiance to the Christian faith have shown such hatred towards Jews. The Christian Gospels unmistakably record not only that Jesus preached a message of love – even for your enemies – but also that He **was** a Jew.

Whilst no one could possibly accuse Jesus of merely accepting without question what was taught by the Jewish leaders of His day, He is documented as piously following Judaism. He often quoted from the Old Testament and, according to Matthew 15:24, He even told a Gentile woman:

> "***I was sent only to the lost sheep of Israel***".

Following our emotional time at the Holocaust Remembrance Centre, we next visited Jerusalem's *Shrine of the Book*, with its unusually shaped round white roof. This interesting building, which is part of the Israel Museum, houses some of the Dead Sea Scrolls.

Although described by Professor F.F. Bruce as being *"the greatest find of twentieth century biblical archaeology"* I confess that, prior to the visit, I had known very little about the Scrolls. We were to learn that, as well as many more recent writings, they contain various copies of all the Old Testament books (apart from the short Book of Esther – one which doesn't mention God and, for whatever reason, isn't ever referred to in the New Testament). Copies of Old Testament books make up around forty per cent of the Scrolls.

The manuscripts of Old Testament books found among the Dead Sea Scrolls are **centuries** older than the oldest which had previously been discovered. Yet, astoundingly, some are almost identical to them. The scribes who meticulously copied these manuscripts down the years maintained an exceptional level of accuracy.

However, there are more copies of some Old Testament books in the Scrolls than of others, and not all the manuscripts of a given book are the same. It is evident that, in the centuries before Jesus, the contents of many Old Testament books were changed. Parts were either altered or deleted and new passages were added. At the time of Jesus there were therefore various **differing** versions of several Old Testament books in circulation. (An example of this can be seen in Luke 4:16-18, where Jesus is quoted as reading from Isaiah 61:1. The wording is noticeably different to what we have in **our** Old Testament.)

A similar situation exists in relation to the New Testament books, which were of course written after the Dead Sea Scrolls. Differences between New Testament manuscripts reveal that it was not uncommon for changes to be made as they were being copied. Some of these changes were simply errors in copying, but others were deliberate. (For example, verses 9-20 of Mark 16 – those verses which describe resurrection appearances of Jesus – are not found in the oldest manuscripts of Mark's Gospel and seem to have been added later.)

Our Israeli guide informed us that the unusual shape of the round white roof of *the Shrine of The Book* is the same as the lids of the jars in which some of the Qumran Scrolls were found and is intended to represent **'the Sons of Light'**.

This term, which occurs frequently in the Scrolls, was used by the Essenes, who dressed in white tunics.

Situated opposite to the white roof of *the Shrine of The Book* is an imposing polished black granite wall representing **'the Sons of Darkness'**, arch enemies of the Essene *'Sons of Light'*.

Sitting down to rest from the mid-day Israeli sun between these two striking symbolic structures remains for me an enduring and emotive memory.

Having earlier in the day visited the immensely moving memorial to the Holocaust, we now found ourselves seated in-between a black wall representing the *'Sons of Darkness'* and a white dome symbolising the *'Sons of Light'*.

It was for me a powerful illustration of the choice we each constantly face in life between the ways of evil and those of goodness, between the ways of hatred and those of love, between the ways of selfishness and those of generosity, between the ways of untruthfulness and those of honesty, between the ways of darkness and those of light.

The term *"children of light"* is used in the New Testament. In Ephesians 5, for example, members of the Christian Church at Ephesus were instructed:

> *Live as **children of light**, for the fruit of the light consists in all goodness, righteousness and truth.*

And **in the problematic Parable of the Unjust Steward in Luke 16, Jesus is quoted as using the very term** *"the sons of light"*, but the meaning is much less obvious:

> *"So the master commended the unjust steward because he had dealt shrewdly. For the sons of this world are more shrewd in their generation than* **the sons of light**. *And I say to you, make friends for yourselves by* **unrighteous mammon**, *that when you fail, they may receive you into an everlasting home."* (Luke 16:8-9, New King James Version)

(The use of both the terms *"the sons of light"* and *"unrighteous mammon"* in this quotation of Jesus is intriguing, and we will be considering the Parable later in the book.)

Surprisingly, however, although the New Testament often refers to Pharisees and to Sadducees, it doesn't contain the word 'Essenes'. No one, it seems, is entirely sure why.

3. JOSEPHUS AND THE ESSENES

The starting point in my quest to find out about the Essenes, I decided, was to read what was written by the Jewish historian Josephus. He has more to say about the sect than any other ancient writer and claims to have had some personal experience of them.

Born in 37AD, just a few years after Jesus' crucifixion, Josephus wrote several books on Jewish history towards the end of the first century. His two main works are *'The Antiquities of the Jews'* (usually referred to simply as 'Antiquities') and *'The Jewish Wars'*.

In one short paragraph in Antiquities 18, Josephus briefly refers to Jesus. In The Jewish Wars, he has a great deal more to say about the Essenes.

As with **all** records, we should not assume that Josephus – a Pharisee who courted Roman approval – was accurate in everything he wrote. There are, no doubt, numerous errors resulting from bias, from exaggeration or from mistake. But much of what he says about the Essenes is confirmed by the contents of the Qumran Scrolls and by other historical sources. For those who would like to read them, his writings are freely available online and I've included a web reference for them (and for my other primary sources) in the Appendix.

The Essenes, according to Josephus, were the third largest Jewish party of the time, the Sadducees were the second, and the Pharisees the largest.

Judaism, however, was fragmented and there were various other groups as well (such as the Zealots, who actively resisted Roman rule, and the Herodians, who are mentioned in Matthew & Mark).

Josephus says the Essenes were themselves divided into different communities, living in various locations, each with differing views on certain issues. This is borne out by the Dead Sea Scrolls.

One Scroll, known as **'the Community Rule'**, copies of which were found **only at Qumran**, speaks of **one** Community – probably being the one based at Qumran.

But another important Scroll, **'the Damascus Document'**, fragments of which have also been found elsewhere, refers to **groups in cities and "*camps*" in different places**.

At the time of Jesus, there were many such Essene communities situated in different locations around the country. There was also possibly one in Egypt.

As I began to read what Josephus records of the Essenes' beliefs, I was immediately struck by several similarities with the teachings of Jesus outlined in the Gospels.

4. ESSENES AND THEIR POSSESSIONS

The origin of the name 'Essenes' is unknown, but it is one which was used by others and not by the Essenes, who regarded of themselves as *'the Sons of Light'* and as *'the Poor'*.

Although, according to Josephus, the sect had many collective possessions, they *"despised"* personal wealth (which they seemingly saw as 'unrighteous mammon') and shared everything together.

On joining, they each handed over all their possessions to be placed in a common fund. As a result, no one suffered the humiliation of abject poverty – having no reason to worry about what they would eat or drink, or what they would wear – and, at the same time, none had the perceived superiority of personal riches.

This commendable practice fits in well with the teachings of Jesus recorded in Matthew 6. Take, for example, the following words found in verses 25-29:

> *"Do not worry about your life, what you will eat or drink, or about your body, what you will wear... See how the flowers of the field grow. They do not labour or spin. Yet I tell you that not even Solomon in all his splendour was dressed like one of these."*

In fact, the Essene attitude to personal property was well summarised by Jesus in verses 19-21:

> *"Do not store up for yourselves treasures on earth... for where your treasure is, there your heart will be also."*

And, exactly like the Essenes, Jesus is quoted in Luke 14:33 as teaching:

> ***"Those of you who do not give up everything you have cannot be my disciples."***

Indeed, it occurred to me that, given the Essenes' identification with the title *'the Poor'*, Essene converts would have seen themselves as doing precisely what Jesus is said in Mark 10:21 to have told a man to do:

> "**Go and sell everything you have and give to the poor**".

In Matthew 13:44 Jesus is recorded as saying:

> *"The kingdom of heaven is like treasure hidden in a field. When a man found it, he hid it again, and then in his joy went and **sold all he had** and bought that field."*

Just as those joining the Essenes did, the man in question sold all he had in order to gain something of much greater value. The same is true of the merchant referred to in the verse which follows:

> *"Again, the kingdom of heaven is like a merchant looking for fine pearls. When he* found *one of great value, he went away and **sold everything he had** and bought it."*

As a result of the challenging requirement to sell your possessions and give the proceeds to a communal fund, taking the decision to enter an Essene community must have been an extremely hard step for a **rich** man to take. The statement of Jesus in Matthew 19:24, "*It is easier for a camel to go through the eye of a needle than for someone who is rich to enter the kingdom of God*", comes readily to mind!

The decision to join an Essene community was not only a potentially difficult one it was also a permanent one. There was to be no going back. They believed, as Jesus is quoted in Luke 9:62 as having taught:

> *"No one who puts his hand to the plough and looks back is fit for service in the kingdom of God".*

Remarkably, the practice of the Essenes regarding their personal property was also that of the first Christians, about whom Acts 4 records the following:

> *All the believers were one in heart and mind. **No one claimed that any of his possessions was his own, but they shared everything they had**.*

> *...there were no needy persons among them for from time to time those who owned lands or houses **sold them**, brought the money from the sales and put it at the apostles' feet, and it was distributed to anyone who had need.*

I had always assumed these early Christians were acting spontaneously. In fact, they were doing what the Essenes did.

Rejecting individual wealth, Essenes had made it their priority to quietly seek righteousness and the coming kingdom of God. They believed, as Jesus is said in Matthew 6:33 to have taught, that you should *"seek first the kingdom of God and His righteousness"* and the necessities of life (such as food and clothing) would be provided.

Matthew 6:24 records Jesus as teaching: *"life does not consist of the abundance of possessions"*. According to Luke 12:14, He went further, uncompromisingly asserting: *"You **cannot** serve both God and money"* (or *"mammon"*). **The Essenes could not have agreed more!**

Most Jewish people of the time saw personal riches as demonstrating **God's blessing** and regarded the poor as having been **cursed** by God. The Essenes had turned this thinking completely **on its head**. In the very same way, Jesus is quoted in Luke 6 as declaring:

> *"**Blessed** are you who are **poor**, for yours is the kingdom of God... But **woe** to you who are **rich**, for you have already received your comfort."*

Luke 12 recounts Jesus' parable of a rich farmer who, having had an abundant harvest, decided he would take life easy and enjoy his wealth, but who was told by God, *"You fool! This very night your life will be demanded from you"*. Nothing is said in Luke about the rich man not having faith in God, but he was planning to build new and bigger barns in which to store his crops. Unlike the Essenes, he was evidently **not** intending to share the food with others.

Meanwhile, Luke 16 – the Chapter in which Jesus is quoted as using the term *"the sons of light"* – relates the sobering parable of another rich man and a beggar. Significantly, the beggar is given a name (Lazarus) but the rich man, who after death found himself in torment, is not. Indeed, we're not told a lot about him, other than that he *"dressed in purple and fine linen"* and *"lived in luxury"*. He had also failed to share his food with Lazarus, who lay at his gate, longing to eat what might fall from his table. Once again, nothing whatever is said about the rich man not exercising faith in God.

Whether they had a faith or not, however, these rich men would have been seen by Essenes as **patently** unrighteous and therefore destined for eternal punishment. Were they righteous men (Essenes would have concluded) they would have handed over all their possessions to the Essene leaders. Thereafter, they would have lived a simple life and certainly not one of luxury. Their food and clothing would have been only what was provided to them by the Essene Community. They would not have worn fine purple clothes. Instead, like the common lilies of the fields, they would have been dressed in **white**.

5. ESSENES AND THEIR PRACTICES

According to Josephus, Essenes dressed in simple white tunics, which were kept until worn out, and a belt. When a member of an Essene Community travelled to another Essene group in a different part of the country, Josephus says, they were welcomed there, being free to share in everything as if one of the Community. As a result, he explains, they did not take anything with them on their journey apart from a staff to defend themselves from attack.

Amazingly, this practice is exactly mirrored in the instructions Jesus is recorded in Mark's Gospel (which is widely thought to be the first Gospel to have been written) as having given the twelve disciples He sent out into the countryside to preach:

> "**Take nothing for the journey except a staff – no bread, no bag and no money in your belts. Wear sandals but not an extra tunic.**" (Mark 6:8).

Admittedly, Luke 9:3 appears to partially contradict Mark, having Jesus tell the disciples to *"take nothing for the journey – **no staff**, no bag, no bread, no money, no extra tunic"*. And according to Matthew 10:10, He instructed them to take *"no bag for the journey, or extra tunic, or sandals, **or a staff**"*. However, Matthew, Mark and Luke are all in agreement that the disciples were told not to take a bag, money, or extra clothing.

Those people living throughout the country who offered hospitality to Jesus' disciples would therefore seem to have provided them not only with a bed and with food but also with clean clothes, just as Essenes did for one another. Might they, I wonder, have been members of Essene communities?

Essene converts had to leave their parents, their brothers and their sisters and go to live in a community. This community became, in effect, their **new** family.

Similarly, Matthew 12:47-49 records the following about Jesus:

> *Someone told him, "Your mother and brothers are standing outside, wanting to speak to you". He replied to him, "Who is my mother, and who are my brothers?"* **Pointing to his disciples, he said, "Here are my mother and my brothers."**

Many parents, no doubt, would have been antagonistic to the idea of their sons and daughters leaving them to go and join an Essene community. Although they taught a message of peace, the Essenes could have accurately said (as Jesus is quoted as doing in Matthew 10:35):

> *"I have come to turn a man against his father, a daughter against her mother, a daughter-in-law against her mother-in-law".*

In the same way as Jesus, Essenes are said to have taught using allegories, or **parables**. And, like Jesus, they engaged in the practice of **healing**. There are numerous references in the Dead Sea Scrolls to healing and some historians even think the name Essenes may have meant "Healers". Josephus claims they used remedies made from roots and other ingredients believed to benefit body and soul.

Another observation made by Josephus is that they got up early in the morning, before the sun had risen, and sought out lonely places, where they would pray. In precisely the same way, according to Mark 1:35,

> *very early in the morning, while it was still dark, Jesus got up, left the house and went off to a solitary place, where He prayed.*

6. ESSENES AND MARRIAGE

Although Jewish Law allowed men to divorce their wives, the Essenes, according to Josephus, were strongly **opposed** to divorce. Apparently sharing the same view, Jesus is quoted in Mark 10:11 as teaching:

> "*Anyone who divorces his wife and marries another woman commits adultery against her.*"

Josephus says Essenes held marriage in disdain and advocated **celibacy**. Some communities did not permit single members to marry, he claims, but others did.

Jesus (who was of course Himself unmarried) is recorded in Matthew 19:12 as saying:

> "*S*ome *are eunuchs because they were born that way; others were made that way by men; and* ***others have renounced marriage*** *because of the kingdom of heaven*".

We are not told to whom Jesus was referring as having renounced marriage, but many Essenes would clearly have fitted the bill. And remarkably, He is quoted as then going on to teach (just as Essenes did):

> *"The one who* ***can*** *accept this* ***should*** *accept it*".

Although this teaching of Jesus may seem to be ignored by many Christians today, it is repeated by the Apostle Paul. In 1 Corinthians 7:8 he writes to the Church in Corinth, "*To the unmarried and to the widows I say: It is good for them to stay unmarried, as I do*". Paul's reasoning is explained in verses 32-34:

> *An unmarried man is concerned about the Lord's affairs – how he can please the Lord. But a married man is concerned about* ***the affairs of this world*** *– how he can please his wife – and his interests are divided.*

Likewise, in a parable of Jesus recounted in Luke 14, a man who was preparing a great banquet had invited many guests, who all began to make excuses as to why they could not attend. One declared, *"I have just bought a field, and must go and see it"*. Another said, *"I have just bought five yoke of oxen, and am on my way to try them out"*. A third announced, *"I have just **got married**, so I can't come"*.

I find it striking that, in line with Essene thinking, the affairs of the world with which these three invitees were regrettably so preoccupied were, in two of the cases, their possessions and, in the third, marriage.

According to Luke 20:34, Jesus taught:

> *"The people of this age marry and are given in marriage. But **those who are considered worthy** of taking part in the age to come and in the resurrection from the dead **will neither marry nor be given in marriage**"*.

Significantly, Jesus is quoted as again using the phrase *"marrying and giving in marriage"* in Matthew 24:38. Warning of God's coming judgement, He told His listeners that it will be like it was in the days of Noah, when the Flood suddenly came and took away those who were *"eating and drinking, marrying and giving in marriage"*.

It would therefore seem from Jesus' teachings that for some of those who perished in the Flood (just as for the third invitee in the parable in Luke 14) getting married was a distraction which proved to have disastrous consequences.

7. ESSENES, OATHS AND ANGER

In Jewish Wars 2.8.7 Josephus outlines the procedure necessary for a man who wished to join the Essenes.

For one year, he says, the applicant was excluded from the Community but had to observe Essene practices. If successful, he then went through a purification ritual with water, not unlike baptism by immersion – the first of many such rituals he would regularly undergo as an Essene.

According to Josephus, the man then entered a two-year apprenticeship, after which he could become a full member.

New members, he claims, had to swear solemn oaths. He sets out what they vowed to do and not do, and we will be looking at these in greater detail in Chapter 20.

A further feature of the Essenes highlighted by Josephus is that they were – in contrast to many people of the time – opposed to the habit of **frequently making oaths**.

In another striking similarity, Jesus is quoted in Matthew 5:34-37 as having taught:

> "But I tell you **do not swear an oath at all**: either by heaven, for it is God's throne; or by the earth for it is his footstool; or by Jerusalem, for it is the city of the Great King. And do not swear by your head, for you cannot make even one hair white or black. All you need to say is simply 'yes' or 'no'."

Some Christians take these words as an outright ban on swearing **any** oaths whatever, such as those taken in a court of law. Many others, however, think Jesus was referring (like the Essenes) to the swearing of oaths in the course of ordinary conversation.

Josephus describes the Essenes as self-controlled and says they thought it a virtue to shun pleasure – something of which Christians have (not infrequently) also been accused!

He regarded them as pious and peaceful folk, who weren't given to expressions of anger with one another. In yet another similarity, Jesus is said in Matthew 5:22 to have taught:

> **"anyone who is angry with a brother or sister will be subject to judgement**... *and anyone who says, 'You fool!' will be in danger of the fire of hell."*

And according to Matthew 6:14-15, He declared:

> *"If you forgive other people when they sin against you, your heavenly Father will also forgive you. But if you do **not** forgive others their sins, your Father will not forgive **your** sins."*

Having read what Josephus records about the beliefs of the Essenes, I began to realise that some of Jesus' teachings may not have been quite as unique as I had always previously assumed.

Take what is commonly known as 'the Sermon on the Mount' in Chapters 5-7 of Matthew's Gospel. Many bible scholars believe these chapters contain a **collection** of Jesus' teachings rather than being just a single sermon. Several of the teachings were also those of the Essenes.

8. THE SERMON ON THE MOUNT

Following on from Jesus' initial message of the need to repent (a point which is often overlooked) the Sermon on the Mount has been widely admired for its literary quality and wisdom.

Some of the concepts and terms used in it – such as *'loving your neighbour as yourself'*, *'turning the other cheek'*, *'going the extra mile'* and *'not letting your left hand know what your right hand is doing'* – have even become part of our everyday speech.

As I read Josephus' writings, I was struck by just how many of the Essene teachings he describes have parallels with those in the Sermon on the Mount. An element of similarity does not mean there was necessarily a direct connection between them. But I increasingly began to question if it could be mere coincidence that so many of Jesus' recorded teachings have so much in common with those of the Essenes.

In the space of two or three pages of Matthew's Gospel, Jesus addresses several of the Essenes' pet subjects. These include the themes of darkness and light, purity of heart, seeking righteousness and not material possessions, food and clothing, divorce, making oaths, expressing anger with your brothers and giving to others.

The Sermon on the Mount commences with the following sayings, or 'Beatitudes':

> *Blessed are the poor in spirit, for theirs is the kingdom of heaven.*
> *Blessed are those who mourn, for they will be comforted.*
> *Blessed are the meek, for they shall inherit the earth.*
> *Blessed are those who hunger and thirst for righteousness, for they will be filled.*
> *Blessed are the merciful, for they will be shown mercy.*
> *Blessed are the pure in heart, for they will see God.*
> *Blessed are the peacemakers, for they will be called children of*

God.
Blessed are those who are persecuted because of righteousness, for theirs is the kingdom of heaven.
Blessed are you when people insult you, persecute you and falsely say all kinds of evil against you because of me. Rejoice and be glad, because great is your reward in heaven, for in the same way they persecuted the prophets who were before you.

These eloquent statements have clear similarities with one of the Dead Sea Scrolls, known as 'the Qumran Beatitudes' or as '4Q525' (shorthand for 'document number 525 from Qumran Cave 4'). In the same way as with the Beatitudes of Jesus, the Qumran Beatitudes comprise eight short statements each beginning with the words *"Blessed are…"*, followed by a ninth much longer one. **Jesus therefore appears to have chosen to employ a poetic style which was used in the Dead Sea Scrolls.**

What is more, the term *"**the poor in spirit**"*, which Jesus uses at the start, is one which is also found in the Scrolls and was evidently used by Essenes. War Scroll 14.7, for example, contrasts *"the poor in spirit"* with *"the hard of heart"*.

Although Psalm 34:18 speaks of the *"crushed in spirit"*, or *"contrite in spirit"*, the Old Testament does not contain the term *"poor in spirit"*. In fact, prior to its use by Jesus, the term is (to the best of my knowledge) one which appeared only in the Qumran Scrolls and not in any other known writings.

9. ESSENE TEACHINGS AND THE LETTER OF JAMES

As with the Sermon on the Mount, several Essene themes are addressed in the New Testament Letter of James. Authorship of James has traditionally been attributed to James, the brother of Jesus mentioned in Galatians 1:19.

James also refers to topics which, according to Josephus, were important to Essenes. Take the question of frequently **swearing oaths**. In the same way as Jesus is recorded as doing, James 5:12 teaches:

> *Above all, my brothers and sisters, do not swear, not by heaven or by earth or by anything else. All you need to say is a simple 'Yes' or 'No'. Otherwise, you will be condemned.*

Adopting a similar attitude as Essenes towards **the rich**, James declares:

> *Believers in humble circumstances ought to take pride in their high position. But the rich should take pride in their humiliation.* (James 1:9)

> *Now listen you rich people, weep and wail because of the misery that is coming to you. Your wealth has rotted, and moths have eaten your clothes... You have lived on earth in luxury and self-indulgence. You have fattened yourselves in the day of slaughter.* (James 5:1-5)

In the same way as Essenes identified with **the poor**, and reflecting the words of Jesus quoted in Luke 6:20, "*Blessed are you who are poor, for yours is the kingdom of God*", James 2:5 asks:

> *Has not God chosen those who are poor in the eyes of the world to be rich in faith and to inherit the kingdom He promised those who love Him?*

And then, as regards the sharing of **food and clothing**, James 2:14-17 poses the following challenging questions:

> *What good is it, my brothers and sisters, if someone claims to have faith but has no deeds? Can such faith save them? Suppose a brother or sister is without clothes or daily food. If one of you says to them 'Go in peace, keep warm and well fed', but does nothing about their physical needs, what good is it? In the same way, faith by itself, if not accompanied by action is dead.*

Placing an emphasis upon the importance of what is **said**, as well as what is done, and in the same way as the Essenes taught members not to express **anger** towards their brothers, James 1:19 teaches:

> *Everyone should be quick to listen, slow to speak and slow to become angry, because human anger does not produce the righteousness that God desires…*

Meanwhile, James 3:5 astutely points out:

> *The tongue is a small part of the body, but it makes great boasts. Consider what a great forest is set on fire by a small spark. The tongue also is a fire, a world of evil among the parts of the body.*

10. THE SECOND TEMPLE PERIOD

Having been impressed by the number of similarities between the teachings of Jesus and those of the Essenes, I concluded that they deserved further investigation. I read many articles and books by a wide variety of different authors on the subjects of the Essenes and the Dead Sea Scrolls, frequently referring back to my primary sources of Josephus, the Scrolls themselves and the Old and New Testaments. This research yielded a lot of fascinating information.

But before I outline any more about the Essenes, it may be helpful if I first try to put it all into an historical **context**. So let us leave *'the Sons of Light'* there for now and take time to consider some of the popular beliefs of Jewish people at the time of Jesus – an era known by historians as the late Second Temple Period.

The **First** Temple Period had ended abruptly back in 597BC, when the Babylonian King Nebuchadnezzar II conquered Jerusalem, destroyed the Temple and took many captives to Babylon. When, 70 years later, the Babylonian Empire was defeated by the Persians, the Persian King Cyrus assisted Jewish exiles to return to Jerusalem and to build the **Second** Temple.

Some two centuries later Jerusalem was again conquered – this time by Alexander the Great and the Greeks. Public worship by Jews came to be forbidden. After a revolt led by the priest Judas Maccabeus, worship in the Temple was restored in 167BC and the Jewish people then regained a degree of independence.

However, with the rise of the Roman Empire, they were conquered yet again. After over a century of Roman rule, and following another rebellion, the Second Temple was destroyed by the Romans in 70AD. A great many of the Jewish people were either slaughtered or dispersed to other lands.

The period of almost 600 years between the building of the Second Temple and its destruction in 70AD is known (logically enough) as the Second Temple Period. It is, of course, towards the end of this Period that Jesus lived.

In around 40BC, a Jewish official named Herod was appointed by the Roman Senate as king, under Roman authority. Known for his ruthlessness, King Herod was unpopular with many of the people. He engaged in several building projects, including commencing a grand extension to the Second Temple. Work on the Temple continued long after his death and was eventually completed only a few years before it was destroyed by the Romans.

Following the death of Herod, his kingdom, according to Josephus, was divided into three. Sons of Herod were appointed to govern each of these regions but, after just a couple of years, two of the sons were removed and replaced by Roman governors. One son, Herod Antipas, remained as the governor of Galilee (the northern area of the country in which Jesus' hometown of Nazareth was situated) and we will be meeting up with him again a little later in the book.

Writings of the Second Temple Period

Biblical scholars think several Old Testament books were either written or compiled in the first half of the Second Temple Period.

Many further books were written by Jewish authors during the **second half** of the Period. Most of these later books are not in the Bible used today by Protestant Churches. But a few of them are included in the Old Testaments of the Roman Catholic Church and/or those of the Russian, Greek and other Orthodox Churches.

(In order to avoid confusion, however, I will in this book be using the term "the Old Testament" to refer to the **Protestant** Old Testament.)

Although not today considered either by Jews or by Protestants as scripture, many of these later books were read by Jews at the time of Jesus. Some were also read by members of the early Christian Church, who clearly believed them to be of value.

For much of my life I've regarded these books as erroneous, whilst asserting that each of the words in the Old Testament (and those in the New Testament) are the words of God Himself. But I had never **read** any of these other books. (Nor, I must confess, was I even aware how or when the Old and New Testaments had been compiled.) I had simply accepted without question what I'd been told by others.

I now recognise that, in doing so, I had not (as I had claimed) put my faith in God alone. Rather, I had placed my faith **in men**: in those who originally penned the Old and New Testament books; in those who subsequently edited them; in those who, in later centuries, selected them for inclusion in the Bible and in those men who had been my Bible teachers.

Of the Old Testament books, copies of the Psalms, Deuteronomy and Isaiah are the most numerous among the Dead Sea Scrolls. (I don't know if it is of significance, but Psalms is the Old Testament book most often recorded in the Gospels as having been quoted by Jesus, Deuteronomy is the second and Isaiah the third.)

In addition to the books of the Old Testament, the Scrolls contain several documents written in the latter half of the Second Temple Period. These include Scrolls known as 'the War Scroll', 'the Temple Scroll', 'Thanksgiving Hymns', 'the Damascus Document' and 'the Community Rule', plus surviving fragments from various other writings. Quite a few of these documents are unique to Qumran.

Also in the Scrolls are several copies of the Book of Tobit and of the Book of Sirach. Although not in the Protestant Bible, these two books are contained in the Old Testaments of the Catholic Church and the Eastern Orthodox Churches.

And then there are numerous copies of certain chapters of **the Book of 1 Enoch**. It is today included in the scriptures of two groups: the Ethiopian Coptic Church (one of the Orthodox Churches) and *Beta Israel* (the Ethiopian Jewish community, who – as their tradition has it – are the descendants of King Solomon and the Queen of Sheba).

Given how many copies of it were discovered among the Qumran Scrolls, 1 Enoch was clearly a popular book with the Essenes, and I will be referring to it again in future chapters.

In the next few chapters, however, I would like to make some observations about the Gospel accounts of the birth of Jesus. These will, I hope, highlight some of the ideas which were around at the time and were central to Essene thinking. They included the concept of an on-going battle between **darkness and light** (a theme often employed in the New Testament). And they included such topics as **stars** (which the Essenes avidly studied), **angels** (the records of whose names the Essenes carefully preserved), **archangels** and **demons**.

11. THE MAGI, KING CYRUS AND THE ZOROASTRIANS

The two Gospel accounts of the Nativity, one found in Matthew and the other in Luke, are so familiar that we tend to take them for granted. A fascinating feature of Matthew's version of events, however, is its story of the visit of the *"wise men"* – or, more correctly, *"magi"* – who followed a shining star.

Foreign travellers were certainly not uncommon in Israel, which was situated on busy trading routes from Eastern lands. It was frequented by many visitors who brought with them their own religions and ideas.

This exposure to other philosophies undoubtedly had an impact upon Jewish society and beliefs.

In the Christian Church, various myths about these *magi* developed over time and it became the tradition there were three of them, supposedly being kings called Melchior, Balthasar and Caspar.

But the Gospel of Matthew doesn't refer to kings, nor does it give their names, or even say how many of them there were. It simply states that they came because they had seen a new star and brought gifts of gold, frankincense and myrrh.

The Greek word used in Matthew 2 and translated in some versions as "*wise men*" is "*magoi*", the plural of *magos*, which I gather is the Greek translation of the Persian word *magus*. **This Persian word does not refer to kings. It refers to Zoroastrian priests.**

The ancient religion of Zoroastrianism, which is known by its followers as '*the Light*', is said to have been founded by Zoroaster – a man whose name (believe it or not) means '*Shining Star*'!

Although Essenes ('*the Sons of Light*') were devout Jews, they had quite a bit in common with followers of Zoroastrianism ('*the Light*').

Not only did Essenes share with Zoroastrians a keen interest in the stars and in angels but, according to Josephus, they also had the reputation of being able to predict future events and to interpret dreams.

Matthew's Gospel could not be said to encourage readers to engage in the practice of astrology. Nevertheless, it is surely striking that, far from seeking to distance Jesus from the beliefs of these foreign astrologers, the Gospel writer readily **accepts** the premise that at least some events **on earth** are related to what happens in **the stars**.

He even goes so far as to assert that these *magi* were **accurate** in their interpretation of the skies. More remarkable still, he says they heard **directly** from God, who warned them in a dream not to return to King Herod.

"Who then were the Zoroastrians?" I perhaps hear you ask. Well, I did too, and so I decided to do a little research. Zoroastrian beliefs, I was to discover, share some notable similarities, not only with those of the Essenes, but also with those of Christians.

Zoroaster, the founder of the religion, is claimed to have lived over 1,000 years BC in Persia (present-day Iran) at a time when people believed there were many gods. At the age of 30, he is said to have experienced a life-changing revelation when he met with the **one** supreme all-wise Lord, whom he recognised to be:

> "*uncreated God, existing eternally and creator of all else that is good*".

In Zoroastrianism, the Lord is assisted by six other holy beings, one of whom is the Holy Spirit. Together, they comprise the seven-fold Spirit of God. For Zoroastrians, therefore, the divine number **seven** is a key one. (Interestingly, the term "*seven spirits of God*" is used in the Book of Revelation – but more on that subject in due course.)

The Lord, according to Zoroastrians, is also assisted by various **angels**, to whom they have given names.

Zoroastrians believe that Ahriman (a name meaning '*The Lie*') is also at work in the world. Aided by **demons**, he seeks to corrupt creation and is destined to be eventually defeated.

Ahriman ('*the Lie*') has much in common with **the Devil** in Christianity who, according to John 8:44, Jesus similarly referred to as "***the father of lies***". Indeed, to my mind, **all** the New Testament references to the Devil have far more in common with Ahriman in Zoroastrianism than they do with the references to Satan found in the Old Testament. Let me explain.

Apart from the Book of Job, which many see as a parable rather than a factual account, there are only two brief Old Testament passages (found in 1 Chronicles 21 and in Zechariah 3) where the name "*Satan*" is used. As a result, Jews today do not believe in Satan as a person or being at all. Rather, they take these references to Satan to represent the inclination towards evil (known in Hebrew as the '*yetzer hara*') existing **in man himself**.

Most ancient religions (including Judaism) required members to follow the practices of their own tradition. But Zoroastrians encourage each **individual** to follow their own God-given conscience. They believe everyone has an immortal soul and, by (1) **good thoughts**, which lead to (2) **good words** and (3) **good deeds**, we all can attain eternal life in paradise. It has even been suggested that the three gifts of the *magi* may have represented these '**three pillars**' of Zoroastrianism.

According to Zoroastrians, there is a great chasm between the living and the dead, and after death each soul crosses the one-way '*Bridge of Separation*' between them. If good thoughts, words and deeds outweigh the bad, it widens, and the soul passes into **paradise**. But if bad thoughts, words and deeds (for which there is no repentance) outweigh the good, the Bridge narrows and the soul falls into **hell**.

The Essenes likewise evidently believed in the existence of an immortal soul, and that the souls of the righteous go to paradise whilst those of the unrighteous are eternally punished.

Another Zoroastrian concept with similarities to the beliefs of the Essenes is that of **the kingdom of God** – a utopian kingdom on earth where goodness prevails, and leaders rule in righteousness and fairness.

This idea of a kingdom of God is illustrated in the approach to leadership which was taken by the Persian **King Cyrus**. He was a Zoroastrian, and it was he who freed the Jewish people from captivity in Babylon, permitting them to return to their homeland.

Unsurprisingly, the Bible speaks well of him, as in the following words at the end of Chapter 44 and beginning of Chapter 45 of Isaiah:

> *I am the Lord... who says of Cyrus, "He is my shepherd and will accomplish all that I please. He will say of Jerusalem, 'Let it be rebuilt' and of the Temple, 'Let its foundations be laid'." This is what the Lord says to **his anointed**, to Cyrus, whose right hand I take hold of to subdue the nations before him...*

King Cyrus, by all accounts, had a very different attitude to leadership from other rulers of the times. In line with Zoroastrian beliefs, he claimed to provide government based on **righteousness and fairness**. This is reflected in an historic object known as 'the Cyrus Cylinder', which was commissioned by him following the conquest of Babylon and is now in the British Museum. The inscription on this ancient clay cylinder – which some historians regard as the first ever charter of human rights – demonstrates that he promoted religious tolerance.

Cyrus allowed subjects to follow their own religions and gave them a significant level of freedom. He permitted Jewish exiles to return to Jerusalem, assisting them to rebuild the Temple and (according to Ezra 1:7) returning the gold and silver articles which had been taken from it by the Babylonians. Josephus says (in Antiquities 11.8) that he even provided **finance** for the project. Such generosity would no doubt have endeared Cyrus to the Jewish people – hence, presumably, the positive reference to him in the above quotation from Isaiah.

Crucially, it is also likely to have influenced the attitude of Jewish people towards such vital concepts as the afterlife, the battle between good and evil, the role of angels and the existence of demons.

Zoroastrianism was very widely practised throughout the Middle East during the Second Temple Period and differed from the religions which had gone before it in the following ways:

1. Zoroastrians held that there is only **one God**, who is good.

2. Believing in the existence of angels and demons, they claimed there is a **battle** continually going on in the world between light and darkness, truth and lies, good and evil, in which light, truth and good will eventually prevail.

3. They believed in the **equality** of all men before God, holding that each individual person – as opposed to their tribe or nation – will be judged in an afterlife according to their thoughts, their words and their actions.

By studying the skies, Zoroastrian priests understood the movement of the sun, moon and planets as a way of measuring the seasons and thus saw them as a means of predicting events. They:

>   (a) studied the **stars**,
>
>   (b) conducted divine **worship** and
>
>   (c) interpreted **dreams**.

So, not only does the word "*magi*" refer to priests who were followers of Zoroaster, but the practices of the *magi* described in Matthew's Gospel – who predicted future events from the stars and from dreams – were indeed those of Zoroastrian priests.

The Essenes, like the Zoroastrians, not only believed in one eternal God and in an on-going battle between good and evil, but they also studied stars and interpreted dreams. In Jewish Wars 2.7, Josephus records that some Essenes predicted the future and interpreted dreams for Herod Antipas, the son of King Herod.

Matthew's remarkable story of the visit of *magi* to the young Jesus affirms the beliefs of both Zoroastrians and Essenes that it is possible to predict some future events by studying the stars (which were seen as messengers) and that God speaks to men through their dreams.

And amazingly, as regards the **priestly roles** of these *magi*, Matthew asserts that they:

(a) **correctly** predicted the birth of Jesus from the stars,

(b) **rightly** worshipped Him and

(c) heard **accurately** from God in their dreams (in which they were warned by God not to return to King Herod).

It is not entirely surprising, then, that some in the Christian Church attempted to reinvent them as 'the Three Kings'!

12. THE BIBLE, ANGELS AND STARS

Luke's account of the birth of Jesus makes no mention of Eastern visitors who followed a shining star. But it famously records the appearance to some shepherds (who were keeping watch over their flocks at night) of an angel and of a great company of "**the heavenly host**".

I find the use of this particular term in Luke 2:13 – especially in relation to a night-time event – most intriguing. Let me try to explain why.

The term "*host of heaven*" (in Hebrew "*tsaba-shamayim*", meaning literally "*army of the skies*") occurs several times in the Old Testament, where it refers to **the stars**. The first mention of the term is in Deuteronomy 4:19, which says:

> ...when you look up to the sky and see the sun, the moon and the stars – all the host of heaven – do not be enticed into bowing down to them and worshipping...

In this passage in Deuteronomy, the host of heaven are defined as being the sun, the moon and the stars (the word "*stars*" presumably intended to include the planets) which are not to be worshipped. The evils of worshipping the sun, moon and stars is a theme repeated time and again in the Old Testament.

I discovered to my great surprise that, throughout the Bible, the words "*stars*" and "*angels*" appear to be interconnected. This is of no little significance as many in ancient times (possibly including the Essenes) believed the stars **to be** angels. Luke's use of the term "*the heavenly host*" does little to discourage the belief!

Neither indeed does Psalm 148:2, when it says:

> Praise him all his **angels**, praise him all his **heavenly hosts**, praise him sun and moon, praise Him all you **shining stars**.

Nor, for that matter, does Job 38:7, when it declares:

> *The morning **stars** sang together, and all the **angels** shouted for joy.*

Nor perhaps does Daniel 12:1-4, which states:

> *At that time **Michael**, the great prince who protects your people will arise…*
>
> *Multitudes who sleep in the dust of the earth will awake, some to everlasting life, others to shame and everlasting contempt. Those who are wise will shine like the brightness of the heavens and those who lead many to righteousness like **the stars** for ever and ever.*

Judges 5 even speaks of stars being engaged in the fighting of battles, implying the "*stars*" referred to were either human or spiritual forces. According to verses 19 & 20:

> *Kings came, they fought… from the heavens **the stars fought**, from their courses they fought against Sisera…*

1 Kings 22:19-21 implies that the host of heaven are indeed **spirits**. The word "*spirits*" is used in the Bible to refer to **angels** (who of course appear at times in human form). In Hebrews 1:14, for example, the writer asks the rhetorical question: "*Are not all angels ministering spirits…?*"

A clear and unmistakable connection between stars and angels is again made in the New Testament.

In Revelation 1:20, **seven stars** seen in a vision by the writer (John of Patmos) "***are the angels***" of seven churches.

Given the widespread belief at the time that the stars of the sky **are** angels, it surely cannot be without significance that John should link seven stars and seven angels in **such** a direct way.

The link between stars and angels is repeated yet again in Revelation 12. It describes the vision of an enormous red dragon which is said to have *"swept a third of the stars"* out of the sky with its tail and to have *"flung them to the earth"*. The third of the stars referred to in this passage in Revelation 12 is widely interpreted as representing angels. Indeed, verse 9 explains that the dragon is:

> *"... that ancient serpent called the devil, or Satan, who leads the whole world astray. He was hurled to the earth **and his angels with him**"*.

In Luke 10:18 Jesus is quoted as saying:

> *"I saw Satan fall like lightning from heaven"*.

And, in the Old Testament, Isaiah 14:12 declares regarding the king of Babylon:

> *"How you have fallen from heaven **morning star**, son of the dawn! You have been cast down to the earth..."*

Revelation may possibly seek to link Isaiah's reference to the fall from heaven of the *"morning star"* with the concept of the fall of Satan from heaven.

But no mention is made, either in Isaiah 14:12 or in Luke 10:18, of the fall of **Satan's angels** to earth (as referred to in Revelation 12).

The coming of disobedient angels to earth is, however, an event which is described in 1 Enoch, the book which was so popular with the Essenes.

Could Revelation 12 perhaps be referring to this story in 1 Enoch? It is outlined in Chapters 6-11, which are among the Chapters of 1 Enoch found in the Dead Sea Scrolls.

As well as telling of fallen angels coming to earth, 1 Enoch contains lots of information about the stars and the planets.

Then, in Chapter 20 (another of the chapters found at Qumran) it lists the **names** of various angels. These include the seven **archangels**, who are named as Gabriel, Michael, Raphael, Uriel, Raguel, Remiel, and Sariel.

Although the Old Testament refers to angels, it isn't until we get to the comparatively recent Book of Daniel that any – Gabriel and Michael – are **named**. Many Jewish (and other) scholars have long since concluded that these names likely came from the Zoroastrians, who named and categorised angels.

It is striking that the Essenes, like the Zoroastrians, studied the stars whilst, at the same time, having a keen interest in angels and their names. Indeed, in Jewish Wars 2.8.5, Josephus says Essenes undertook to carefully preserve *"the books of their sect and the names of the angels"*.

13. ANGELS AND ARCHANGELS

In Revelation, John of Patmos not only recounts a vision of seven *"stars"* that were seven *"angels"* but (in Revelation 8:2) declares:

> *"I saw the seven angels who stand before God..."*

This would seem to be a reference to the **seven archangels** as, in very similar wording, the Book of Tobit (with which John would probably have been familiar and which is included in the Qumran Scrolls and in the Bibles of the Catholic and Orthodox Churches) describes the archangel Raphael as being:

> *"...one of the seven who stand before the Lord..."* (Tobit 12:15)

Some people of the times believed the so-called **"seven planets"** – a term referring to the Sun, the Moon and the five planets visible to the naked eye (Mercury, Venus, Mars, Jupiter & Saturn) – **were the seven archangels**.

Although the word "archangel" is not used in the Old Testament, archangels **are** mentioned in the New.

Luke's Gospel tells of visits of Gabriel to the Virgin Mary and to Zechariah (the father of John the Baptist) and the word *"archangel"* is used on two occasions.

1 Thessalonians 4:16 says that *"the voice of the archangel"* will herald Christ's Second Coming, and in the Book of Jude, there is a reference to the archangel Michael. Verse 9 of Jude speaks of an episode, not mentioned anywhere else in the Bible, when Michael is said to have had a dispute with the Devil about the body of Moses.

These New Testament verses appear to me to have much more in common with 1 Enoch than they do with the books of the Old Testament.

As well as mentioning archangels, the New Testament frequently refers to angels.

The Book of Acts and each of the New Testament Gospels record the appearance of angels at various times. And Jesus is quoted as talking of angels in connection with His return, such as in Matthew 25:31:

> *"When the Son of Man comes in his glory, and all **his angels** with him, he will sit on his glorious throne".*

According to the accounts of Jesus' resurrection in Matthew 28 & John 20, one or more angels were present at the tomb. (Mark 16, however, does not use the word 'angel' but instead speaks of "*a young man dressed in a white robe*", whilst Luke 24 refers to "*two men*").

And John 5:4 tells of the popular belief in an angel who at times *"troubled the waters"* of the Pool of Bethesda in Jerusalem, leading to miraculous healings. (I should, however, point out that this verse is seemingly not found in the oldest manuscript we have of John's Gospel and may therefore be another later addition.)

It is evident that, in the late Second Temple Period, there was in Jewish society – and particularly among the Essenes – a keen interest in angels. Along with this interest in angels, there was (in common with the Zoroastrians) a widespread belief in demons.

14. DEMONS AND ILLNESS

Demons (as with angels and archangels) are referred to in the Dead Sea Scrolls. In 11 Qumran Psalms 27, for example, wording is suggested for use when driving demons out of those who are ill.

Whilst there is a curious reference in 1 Samuel 16:14 to *"an evil spirit from the Lord"* which tormented King Saul, the concept of casting out demons **is not** one found in the Old Testament. Yet, when we come to the **Gospels**, we find **numerous** references to demons, and their role in illness would seem to be taken for granted by the writers.

As the Old Testament doesn't mention demons, most Jews today do not believe in their existence. At the time of Jesus, however, there was a widely held belief in Jewish society that demons were a significant cause of sickness. This is confirmed by Josephus, who himself believed in demons which bring about illness. In Jewish Wars 7.6.3, he describes them as being (in his understanding) the spirits of wicked men who had died and which "*enter into men that are alive and kill them*".

The New Testament Gospels (except for the Gospel of John) testify to Jesus having often cast out demons, mostly in connection with **healing**. But the practice was not unique to Jesus and His disciples.

Matthew 12 says that some Pharisees thought Jesus was exorcising demons through the power of "*Beelzebub*" (a name meaning *"Lord of the Flies"*, which presumably referred either to a leading demon or to Satan himself). According to verse 27, Jesus asked them:

> "*If I drive out demons by Beelzebub, by whom do **your people** drive them out?*"

This question clearly implies there were **other** Jewish people of the time who were **also** perceived as having cast out demons.

Present-day Christians are divided on the issue of demons and their connection with sickness. Some don't take the Gospel references to demons literally, instead seeing them as a first century way of describing some medical conditions, such as epilepsy or mental illness.

Indeed, the symptoms of a demonised boy described in Mark 9 are much like those of epilepsy. And a distressed man in Mark 5, who was self-harming, who could not be restrained, and whose demons are said to have gone into a herd of pigs, would today be regarded as being mentally ill. Interpretating the Gospels in this way, however, would appear to seriously question their accuracy.

Some other Christians believe in the existence of demons but consider them irrelevant to present-day illness; others hold that demons remain active today and can cause sickness; and then there are some who would seem to see demons at almost every turn. But such beliefs do not have much accepted scientific evidence to support them; nor do they accord with recognised medical practice. (See, however, the Book *'Demonic Foes: My 25 Years as a Psychiatrist Investigating Possessions, Diabolic Attacks and the Paranormal'* by Dr Richard Gallagher.)

15. SADDUCEES AND PHARISEES

Not all Jews in the late Second Temple Period believed in the existence of demons. One major group who certainly did not were **the Sadducees**.

Josephus says the Sadducees were a wealthy and powerful elite who were mainly concerned with the affairs of the Temple in Jerusalem. They saw themselves as keeping true to the **original** faith of their ancestors, unpolluted by the theories of men and by foreign religions such as Zoroastrianism, with its devil (Ahriman), its demons and its fixation with angels and stars.

Sadducees denied the existence of **any** spiritual realm and recognised only the **physical** world. They did not believe in an immortal soul or in life after death. Neither did they believe in the existence of angels or demons.

They presumably took the angels referred to in the Old Testament to be **human** messengers, as the Hebrew word for angel simply means "messenger". Or perhaps they saw angels as being a manifestation of God Himself (as with the angel who is said in Judges 13 to have appeared to Manoah and his wife, whose name was *"beyond understanding"* and about whom Manoah exclaimed: *"**We have seen God!**"*).

Josephus records that Sadducees placed most emphasis on *"the Law of Moses"* – the Books of Genesis, Exodus, Leviticus, Numbers and Deuteronomy. They seemingly treated the writings of the Old Testament prophets with some scepticism and totally rejected the later Book of Daniel, all the additional books of the Essenes and the unwritten traditions of the Pharisees.

Being primarily concerned with the ceremonies of the Temple, Josephus claims, Sadducees regarded life outside the Temple as largely irrelevant to their religion and were happy to co-operate with the Romans. They were seen by many other Jews as elitist – or as just plain snobbish – and as being much too friendly with the Roman occupiers.

According to Josephus, Sadducees did not believe in fate and didn't share the expectation of a coming Messiah. They no longer had a role to play after the Temple was destroyed in 70AD and would appear to have ceased to exist as a distinct group not long after that.

Not mincing his words, John the Baptist is said in Matthew 3:7 to have called the Sadducees and Pharisees "*a brood of vipers*" – a sentiment the Essenes would likely have endorsed! Matthew 12:34 quotes Jesus as using the same term. (Presumably Jesus borrowed it from John, or perhaps the term was also used by others, such as Essenes.)

Jesus accused the Sadducees of neither knowing scriptures nor appreciating God's power in denying a future resurrection of the body. He also criticised the "*teachers of the Law*", a term which may well have included Sadducees. However, He is not recorded as criticising them quite as often as He did **the Pharisees**.

Pharisees were the largest party of Jews at the time and are effectively the forefathers of modern Judaism. Although not an aristocratic elite, they saw themselves as a **righteous** elite.

In around 150BC, the Pharisees (whose name means "*Separatists*") had formed a club, or association, whose members were required to observe strict rules and to maintain separation from those regarded as 'sinners'. Communal meals played a big part in Jewish social and religious life, and Pharisees were very choosy about those with whom they would share their meals.

Whilst the Sadducees were mainly concerned with the worship and sacrifices of the Temple in Jerusalem, Pharisees had set up local synagogues around the country for study of the Jewish Law.

They followed their own Oral Law (which was unwritten at the time of Jesus but was mostly added to the written Jewish Talmud by the second century AD). Interpreting and expanding the Old Testament scriptures, they had added many rules and regulations to the 'Law of Moses'.

Unlike Sadducees, Pharisees believed in the existence of an immortal soul, which lives on after death in the depths of the earth. They held that, on 'the Last Day', there will be a physical resurrection of the bodies of righteous Jews, which will then be reunited with their souls.

So, in the Jewish society into which Jesus was born, the topic of **resurrection** was one which was vigorously debated. An example of this can be seen In Acts 23, when the Apostle Paul was brought before the Jewish ruling Council, the Sanhedrin. Paul (who was a Pharisee by birth) claimed he had effectively been put on trial because of his belief in the resurrection of the dead. A heated argument then broke out between those in the Sanhedrin who were Pharisees, who believed in resurrection, and those who were Sadducees and did not.

For Pharisees, however, the concept of a future bodily resurrection was not so much connected with **personal** salvation as with the collective redemption of the Jewish **nation** and the restoration of creation by God.

They believed in and longed for the coming of a righteous king, *'the Messiah'*, who would rule in majesty over the whole nation as King David had once done. But they simply couldn't entertain the possibility that someone who failed to keep every detail of Jewish Law (as they interpreted it) and who, as Jesus did, associated with 'sinners' **could** be the Messiah.

The Pharisees, like the Essenes, had been founded in the late Second Temple Period, **after** the exposure of the Jewish people to the philosophies of the Zoroastrians and the Greeks.

The beliefs of the Sadducees – which weren't based upon the existence of a spiritual realm or of a life after death – appear, on the other hand, to have had **earlier** beginnings. This would seem to be reflected in the contents of the Old Testament. Let me explain what I mean.

Not only does the Old Testament not use the terms "archangels" or "demons", but it is an inescapable fact that very few (if indeed any) of

its 23,000 verses make a clear and unambiguous reference to the existence of an afterlife.

Exodus 3 contains the Divine declaration, "*I am the God of your fathers, the God of Abraham, the God of Isaac and the God of Jacob*", upon which Jesus is recorded as having commented:

"*He is not God of the dead but of **the living***" (Matthew 12:27).

However, whilst Abraham, Isaac and Jacob (and a few others) are described in the Old Testament as having on death been *"gathered"* to their *"people"*, these ambiguous words are not **explained**.

The concept of an immortal soul which after death lives on either in heaven or in hell (as believed by the Zoroastrians, by the Essenes, and of course by a great many Christians) **is not set out in the Old Testament**.

Perhaps the closest it comes to doing so is in the later-written Book of Daniel. Reference is made in Daniel 12 to "*multitudes who sleep in the dust of the earth*" **awakening**, either to "*everlasting life*" or to "*everlasting contempt*".

Meanwhile, Isaiah 14:9 speaks of *"spirits of the departed"* being **roused** to greet the king of Babylon in *"the realm of the dead below"*.

And, in 1 Samuel 28, King Saul gets a witch to "***bring up***" the dead prophet Samuel. (This story in 1 Samuel is thought by some to be at odds with the teaching of Jesus in Luke 16:26 that there is a *"great chasm"* fixed between the dead and the living which cannot be crossed – teaching not dissimilar to that of the Zoroastrians.)

These Old Testament passages lend support to the Pharisees' theory that the souls of the dead are in the depths of the earth, from where they can presumably be 'brought up' by a medium. But these passages would appear to me to raise (no pun intended!) more **questions** than to make any clear-cut statement about life after death.

Individual verses in Psalm 49, Isaiah 26 and Hosea 13 refer to the righteous being "*redeemed*" or "*delivered*" from the grave.

However, much of the Old Testament – including several lengthy parts describing God's coming judgement upon the wicked – remains remarkably silent on the crucial topic of life after death.

At the same time, it places a **great** deal of emphasis upon **this** life and events on earth – a fact that Sadducees in their debates with Pharisees were no doubt keen to point out.

Understandably, many scholars regard the belief in an afterlife as a **later addition** to Jewish theology which came from the ideas of the Zoroastrians, the Greeks and others.

And it isn't surprising that Jews today, whilst believing in life after death, place greater emphasis – as the Old Testament so obviously does – on life in the here and now.

Although believing in an afterlife, the Pharisees could be viewed as 'small picture' people who were so concerned with the detail of Jewish Law they had lost sight of the bigger picture. Keeping strictly to the **letter** of the Law, they were meticulous in their religious practices.

Take as an example the practice of tithing – one which goes back as far as Abram, who is said in Genesis 14:20 to have given "*a tenth of everything*" to a priest named Melchizedek.

Pharisees apparently went so far as to set aside exactly one tenth of **everything** – not simply of their overall income but of every separate item they produced, such as, for example, of each different spice grown in a herb garden!

The Pharisees' teachings were therefore centred on the need for correct (or 'lawful') actions. This differed from the Zoroastrian emphasis, which was shared by the Essenes, on the 'three pillars' of good thoughts, good words and good deeds. I find it striking that, when criticising the

Pharisees, Jesus is recorded as stressing, just as the Essenes and the Zoroastrians did, the central priority of righteousness in your thoughts (in other words in your mind, or "*heart***") and in word (your *"mouth"*) and not merely in actions alone.**

Here are some examples taken from the Gospel of Matthew:

> *"Why do you entertain evil thoughts in your **hearts**?"*

> *"You have heard that it was said, 'Do not commit adultery', but I tell you that anyone who looks at a woman lustfully has already committed adultery with her in his **heart**."*

> *"Where your **treasure** is, there will your **heart** be also."*

> *"A **good** man brings good things out of the good stored up in **his heart**, and an **evil** man brings evil things out of the evil stored up in **his heart**. For the **mouth** speaks what the **heart** is full of."*

> *"What goes into someone's mouth does not defile them. But what comes **out of their mouth** that is what defiles them."*

> *"For out of the **heart** come **evil thoughts** – murder, adultery, sexual immorality, theft, false testimony, slander. These are what defile a person."*

> *"Woe to you teachers of the law and Pharisees. You hypocrites! You are like whitewashed tombs, which look beautiful on the outside but on the **inside** are full of the bones of the dead and everything unclean."*

> *"Woe to you teachers of the law and Pharisees. You hypocrites! You give a tenth of your spices – mint, dill and cumin. But you have neglected the more **important** matters of the law – justice, mercy and faithfulness."*

Jesus is recorded as having frequently criticised the Pharisees. They were roundly condemned by Him for placing unreasonable burdens on the shoulders of the people, for self-righteous arrogance and for a lack of proper perspective.

But, although Jesus had a great deal more in common with the theology of the Pharisees than He did with that of the Sadducees, the Gospels contain **fewer** (albeit no less vehement) criticisms by Him of the Sadducees. **Why**, then, is this the case?

It would presumably have been obvious to most people that Jesus disagreed with the Sadducees on such crucial issues as the existence of an immortal soul and an afterlife. (Indeed, such fundamental differences make today's theological disagreements between Catholics and Protestants, or between Calvinists and Pentecostals, seem trivial.)

It may therefore have been more important for Jesus to make clear that, whilst He agreed with the Pharisees on these fundamental issues, He was nevertheless opposed to many of their practices and priorities.

It is also possible Jesus criticised the Sadducees much more often than has been recorded. The Gospel writers were not attempting to give a complete account of Jesus' life and teachings but were instead each **selecting** certain sayings and events. As the party of Sadducees had largely died out by the time the Gospels were written, recording Jesus' criticism of them would have been less relevant for the writers than were His denunciations of the Pharisees.

Meanwhile, as far as the Essenes are concerned, there is no record of Jesus having ever mentioned them by name (apart, that is, from His reference in the Parable of the Unjust Steward to *"the sons of light"*).

Different suggestions have been made as to why this is.

1. The Essenes, some have suggested, being a smaller and divided denomination, might not have been considered by Jesus as worthy of mention (even though He agreed with so much of their thinking).

2. As the Gospels were not written until some decades after Jesus' ministry, criticism by Him of the Essenes could perhaps have been interpreted by the writers as criticism of the Pharisees. (The Essenes might even have been regarded as a sub-division of the Pharisees.)

3. Jesus, some claim, was **Himself** an Essene and therefore didn't use the name 'Essenes', but (as Essenes did) strongly criticised both the Sadducees and the Pharisees.

So, let us now look at some more of what is known about the Essenes and their beliefs.

16. ESSENES, AUTHORITY AND ROMAN COINS

The Dead Sea Scrolls indicate that the Essene sect was founded somewhere between 200BC and 150BC and was later led by a man known as *"the Teacher of Righteousness"*. He and others had split from the rest of the priesthood in Jerusalem, becoming involved in a bitter dispute with another Jewish leader, who is referred to in the Scrolls as *"the Wicked Priest"*.

Setting up a community in the desert at Qumran (on the site of what had possibly once been a military fort) the Essenes saw themselves as righteous rivals to the official Temple regime in Jerusalem. They viewed it as corrupt and as engaging in improper practices.

Believing they were chosen by God, Essenes regarded themselves not only as *'the Sons of Light'* and as *'the Poor'* but also as **'the Elect'** – a term frequently used in the Book of 1 Enoch. Jesus is recorded in both Mark 13 and Matthew 24 as likewise using the word *"elect"*, and it is of course found in various books of the New Testament. The Letter of 1 Peter is even addressed to *"God's Elect"* and, as with the Sermon on the Mount and the Letter of James, includes several teachings which were also those of the Essenes.

1 Peter 2:13-14, for example, contains the instruction: *"Submit yourselves for the Lord's sake to every human authority: whether to the emperor, as the supreme authority, or to governors who are sent by him"*. Essenes similarly believed in being subject to all those who are in government. According to Josephus, their reasoning was that no one can have **achieved** a position of authority without **God's** sovereign assistance. Their logic was the same as the Apostle Paul when he wrote:

> *Everyone must submit himself to the governing authorities, for there is no authority except that which God has established.* (Romans 13:1)

The third century Christian historian Hippolytus says that some Essenes did not engage in any trade. Nor, it seems, did they use Roman coins. The coins were seen by some Jews as having on them *"graven images"* in breach of the second of the Ten Commandments. They of course bore images of the heads of the Caesars, who were regarded as gods.

Given the belief in being subject to those in authority, however, it must be assumed that Essenes **would** have paid their poll-tax. There was, of course, little choice – payment was forcefully demanded by the Roman authorities.

Matthew 22 tells of an occasion when some Pharisees asked Jesus: *"Is it right to pay the poll-tax to Caesar or not?"* – a trick question, if ever there was one! Requesting one of the coins used to pay the tax, Jesus asked them whose **image** and whose inscription appeared on it. *"Caesar's"*, they of course replied. (The significance of the use of the word *"image"* in Jesus' question would surely not have been lost on His inquisitors.) He is quoted as then giving His superb response to their trick question:

> ***"So, give back to Caesar what is Caesar's and to God what is God's"*** (Matthew 22:21).

These words of Jesus could be seen as eloquently summarising the practice of using coins with the image of Caesar for the sole purpose of paying Roman taxes. Indeed, the Essenes could hardly have put it any better themselves!

17. QUMRAN COMMUNITY LIFE

Members of Essene communities, according to Josephus, rose early in the morning to have a quiet time of individual prayer.

Following morning prayers, he records, they diligently attended to whatever work they had each been assigned until mid-day, when they would assemble and ritually bathe in cold water.

Next, they quietly entered a dining hall, where they were each given food. Only when one of the Community leaders had given thanks to God for the food did they begin to eat.

After the meal, they returned to their work until evening, when they would again assemble, wash, and dine in the same way.

Josephus' description of Essene community life fits in well with what has been discovered from archaeological exploration at Qumran. The size and nature of the ruins indicate that a community of up to 200 people may have lived there.

One large room has been identified as being the dining hall. The discovery by French archaeologist and priest Roland de Vaux of plates, bowls, jugs and other crockery in an adjoining store would seem to confirm the room was indeed used for dining (see *'Archaeology and the Dead Sea Scrolls'* by Roland de Vaux).

Another large room at Qumran is thought likely to have been a communal meeting room.

And the remains of ancient inkwells found in a third large room would suggest it was the one in which scribes, sitting at huge tables, would have carefully copied the Old Testament and other Essene Scrolls.

Excavations also reveal that the buildings contained an elaborate system for the storage and supply of water, which would have been necessary for the regular bathing Josephus describes. There are rooms with steps leading down from the entrance to a lower floor-level, which could well have been used for this purpose.

Meanwhile, a study in 2011 of some 200 textile fragments found at Qumran conducted by the Israel Antiquities Authority found them to be made of white linen. This is consistent with Josephus' description of the Essenes as having worn white tunics. (In contrast, coloured clothing made from wool was the most common form of dress in the Jewish society of the late Second Temple Period.)

As for the claim made by Hippolytus that some Essene groups did not engage in any trade, archaeologists have discovered evidence at Qumran of the existence of a mill for grinding grain and of a potter's workshop.

Some think these were commercial in nature and were used to manufacture and sell flour and items of pottery for profit. Given the relatively remote desert location of the site, however, most experts believe the mill and pottery were much more likely part of the infrastructure of an exclusive and self-sufficient Essene community.

Community Rule 8.1 indicates that the Qumran Community was headed by a governing Council consisting of three priests and **twelve** of the members, one member for each of the twelve tribes of Israel.

But although Essene communities had a strict leadership structure, Josephus claims they held communal **votes** on some matters.

And he says they taught that those in positions of leadership **must not abuse** the authority they have been given.

The Essene teaching that those in positions of authority were not to abuse them was not dissimilar to the Zoroastrian principle of leaders who rule in righteousness and fairness.

In much the same way as both, Jesus is recorded in Mark 10 as telling His disciples:

> *"You know that those who are regarded as rulers of the Gentiles **lord it over them**, and their high officials exercise authority over them. **Not so with you**. Instead, whoever wants to become great among you must be your servant."*

Damascus Document 9 says a member of an Essene community should not bring to the leaders a complaint against a fellow member unless he had first **spoken to him** about the matter in the presence of some **others**.

Remarkably, in another striking parallel, Jesus is quoted in Matthew 18:15-17 as having likewise taught:

> ***"If your brother or sister sins, go and point out their sin, just between the two of you. If they listen to you, you have won them over. But if they will not listen, take one or two others along, so that every matter may be established by the testimony of two or three witnesses. If they still refuse to listen, tell it to the church."***

Jewish Law required certain allegations to be confirmed by two or more witnesses. Numbers 35:30 says that a person should not be sentenced to death for murder on the evidence of any less than two people; and in Deuteronomy 19:15, the same principle is applied to convictions for other crimes.

These, however, were legal rules of evidence. The instructions of Jesus quoted above, on the other hand, relate to the way in which a dispute between two **church** members should be handled. The principle outlined by Jesus was essentially the same as that in the Damascus Document for a dispute between two members of an **Essene** community.

According to Josephus, Essenes who had been found guilty of committing a serious offence were expelled. As a result of having taken a vow to eat **only** the food provided to them by the Community, he claims, those who were expelled were not free to accept any food which came from other people.

Just such a rule is contained in Community Rule 5.15. It instructed members not to eat anything which came from outsiders. [As Essenes shared both food and clothes, it is possible this would have applied to their clothing as well.]

Josephus explains that Essenes who were expelled from the Community, but who stayed true to their solemn vow not to accept food from non-Essenes, ended up eating grass and such like.

When almost starving, he records, they often would, out of compassion, be accepted back into the Community, being deemed to have endured enough punishment.

18. EDUCATION, TOILETS AND THE SABBATH

Although much of the day-to-day work carried out by Essenes would have been manual, they had a high regard for education. They were all schooled in the Old Testament and other Essene books.

The first century historian Philo of Alexandria (in a book known as *'Every Good Man is Free'*) records the following:

> *In these they are instructed at all other times, but particularly on the seventh day. For that day has been set apart to be kept holy and on it they abstain from all other work and proceed to sacred places they call synagogues.*
>
> *There, arranged in rows, the younger below the elder, they sit quietly, as befits the occasion, with attentive ears. Then one takes the book and reads aloud, and another of special proficiency comes forward and expounds what is not understood. For most of their philosophical study takes the form of allegory* [or parables] *and in this they follow the traditions of the past.*
>
> *They are trained in piety, holiness, justice, domestic and civil conduct, knowledge of what is truly good, or evil, or indifferent, and how to choose what they should do and avoid the opposite.* **They take for their defining standards these three: love of God, love of virtue, and love of humankind.**

These three defining Essene principles, of course, feature prominently in the teachings of Jesus outlined in the Gospels, especially those in the Sermon on the Mount.

According to Josephus, Essenes each carried an implement, which would seem to have been a bit like a garden trowel. On days other than the Sabbath, he says, they would seek out a remote place, where they would dig a hole to use a toilet, which they then filled in.

He records (in Jewish Wars 8) that Essenes had stricter Sabbath rules than other Jews, even going so far as to avoid defecating on the Sabbath. This appears to be borne out by two of the Scrolls. Damascus Document 10.21 instructs members to walk **no further than 1,000 cubits** (about 500 metres) from the camp on the Sabbath. Alas, it was also a requirement, outlined in War Scroll 7.7, that latrines were to be situated **more than 2,000 cubits** from the camp!

Such a location for the latrines has indeed been confirmed by excavations at Qumran in 2006 by the Hebrew University of Jerusalem. (I don't know how quickly an Essene could run the 2,000 cubits at sunset and can only guess as to the likely length of the queue for the latrines on a Saturday night in Qumran!) Surprisingly, the Qumran buildings also seem to have contained an internal toilet – perhaps for use in emergencies.

Josephus makes a curious reference in Jewish Wars 8.9 to Essenes covering themselves when going to the toilet, so as not to offend the "*divine*" rays of the sun. It is **extremely** unlikely that such pious Jews as the Essenes would have engaged in any kind of sun worship. (The Old Testament's emphatic prohibition of worshipping the "*host of heaven*" is indeed repeated in Temple Scroll 55.17.) So, to what could Josephus have possibly been referring?

I would venture to suggest that the passing reference made by Josephus to Essenes having regarded the sun's rays as "*divine*" might perhaps relate to the belief in the Sun as one of the **seven archangels**. Whilst not worshipped, archangels would presumably have been treated with reverence as esteemed messengers of God.

19. DEATH, BURIAL AND RESURRECTION

Both the Essenes and the Pharisees believed each person has an immortal soul. But from what is said by Josephus, who was himself a Pharisee, it appears the belief was of much greater importance for Essenes.

Pharisees (as the Old Testament does) placed most emphasis on this life on earth. Essenes, on the other hand, regarded mortal life as of little value compared to the future glory of an eternal life in heaven (as in New Testament teaching). Consequently, Josephus explains, they saw death as being **better** than life.

He recounts in Jewish Wars 2.153 how, when some Essenes were being brutally killed by Roman soldiers, they **rejoiced** in the future glory awaiting them and, *"smiling in their pain"*, they *"gave up their souls cheerfully"*. Such a positive attitude to death may have seemed very odd to Romans and to many Jews. But it is the same as that of the Apostle Paul, when he declares in Philippians 1 that "*to die is gain*" and to be with Christ in glory is "***better by far***".

Essenes, according to Josephus, believed death to be a victorious release, when the soul is **immediately** set free to rise upwards, rejoicing. He claims they held that the souls of the righteous find a home beyond the seas in paradise – a place refreshed by gentle breezes – whilst the souls of the unrighteous go to a place of never-ending punishment.

In the light of what is said by Josephus about this Essene belief, it is remarkable that Jesus is quoted in Luke 23:43 as telling one of those was crucified along with Him:

*"Truly I tell you, **today** you will be with me in **paradise**"*.

And elsewhere in the Gospels (such as, for example, in Matthew 25:46) Jesus is recorded as having warned of eternal punishment for the unrighteous.

The historian Hippolytus (in Chapter 22 of the book '*Philosophumena IX*') asserts that the Essenes believed in a future **resurrection** of the bodies of the righteous, which will then become immortal:

> *The doctrine of the resurrection has also derived support among them, for they acknowledge both that the flesh will rise again and that it will be immortal.*

As with the Old Testament, not much is said in the Dead Sea Scrolls about resurrection. And Josephus makes no mention of Essenes having shared the belief in resurrection (although neither does he claim they rejected it, as the Sadducees did). Archaeological investigation at Qumran, however, reveals that those who lived there had uncommon burial practices. Most Jews were interred along with family members, either in graves in the ground or – in the case of wealthier families – in tombs hewn out of rock. **But many at Qumran have been buried in individual graves which are aligned to face north to south** (see '*Archaeology and the Dead Sea Scrolls*' by Roland de Vaux). It would seem likely, as with numerous other religious groups who align their graves in one direction, that this practice related to the belief in a future resurrection.

Following Jesus' crucifixion, according to Mark 15, His body was taken by a prominent member of Jewish society named Joseph of Arimathea and placed in a tomb cut out of rock. Some have speculated that, if Jesus was an Essene, members of the sect may have taken the body for burial in a grave in the ground which was (in their view) correctly aligned in readiness for resurrection on 'the Last Day'. There is little evidence to support such a theory, but Mark 16:5 does refer to "*a young man dressed in a white robe*" seen at the tomb.

20. JOSEPHUS AND THE ESSENE OATHS

In Jewish Wars 2.8, Josephus says someone who wished to join the Essenes was required to swear *"awesome oaths"*. These were:

> To piously love God, to cherish justice to all men, and to cause harm no one,
>
> to love the righteous [in other words his brothers, *'the Sons of Light'*],
>
> to hate the wicked [*'the Sons of Darkness'*],
>
> to be subject to all those who are in authority,
>
> not to abuse whatever authority he himself is given,
>
> not to seek to outdo others in dress or finery,
>
> to always love the truth and reprove those who lie,
>
> to refrain from theft and from *"unlawful gain"*,
>
> not to conceal anything from other members of the group,
>
> only to communicate doctrines in the same way he received them,
>
> not, even on threat of death, to disclose any **secret** doctrines to outsiders,
>
> to preserve the Essene books and their records of the names of angels.

The Community Rule does not refer to these specific vows, merely stating that each new member must *"swear a binding oath to return to the Law of Moses"*. The first Chapter, however, outlines the main principles of the Community, and they have numerous similarities with the oaths Josephus describes. The issues of loving justice, hating the unjust, respecting those in authority and not abusing whatever authority you are given are all common themes, as are those of loving the truth, detesting lies and refraining from unlawful gain.

The oath described by Josephus not to conceal anything from other members of the Community is reflected in Community Rule 8.12. Regarding new members, it says: *"Let nothing of that which was hidden from Israel, but found by the man who seeks, be hidden from them"*. And in much the same way as Josephus talks of keeping certain doctrines secret from outsiders, Community Rule 4 instructs members to keep hidden **"*the secrets of knowledge*"**. (I will be returning to the fascinating subject of the Essenes and their secrets once again in Chapter 38.)

The Essene vow to preserve their ancient books and the names of angels, underlines the importance they placed on angels and on the Essene books, especially the Book of 1 Enoch. The chapters of 1 Enoch which list angels' names are included in the Dead Sea Scrolls. The fact the Scrolls remained largely undisturbed in caves at Qumran for nearly 2,000 years shows **just how** seriously Essenes took their safekeeping.

And Community Rule 1.11 confirms the Essene teaching to love the righteous *'Sons of Light'* but hate the wicked *'Sons of Darkness'*. This teaching, it would appear, is one which **Jesus pointedly contradicted**.

21. JESUS AND THE ESSENES

Like Essenes, Jesus: engaged in healing; remained celibate; was critical of both the Sadducees and Pharisees; rose early in the morning; prayed in solitary places; gave thanks before meals; used parables; referred to God as *"Father"*; spoke of angels and of paradise and, when sending out disciples, told them (at least, according to Mark's Gospel) not to take any money, food, or extra clothing, but only a staff.

And several of the recorded teachings of Jesus have noticeable similarities with the beliefs of the Essenes outlined by Josephus, such as: His advocating love for your brothers, selling and sharing your possessions, and being celibate; His identification with the poor; His warnings of God's judgement and of eternal punishment; and His preaching against divorce, anger, materialism, making frequent oaths and lording it over others. **However, there would seem to be the following contrasts between His teachings and those of (at least some of) the Essenes.**

1. Hating Enemies

Jesus is quoted in Matthew 5:43-45 as contradicting the requirement in the Qumran Community Rule to love your brothers and hate your opponents, telling His listeners:

> *"You have heard that it was said, 'Love your neighbour and hate your enemy'. But I tell you, **love your enemies** and pray for those who persecute you, that you may be children of your father in heaven".*

Unlike other statements referred to by Jesus in the Sermon on the Mount and preceded by the words *"you have heard that it was said"*, the instruction to hate your enemies is not found in the Old Testament. Both the writings of Josephus and the contents of the Community Rule indicate that it was the Qumran Essenes who taught this.

In the Sermon on the Mount, Jesus taught a great deal with which Essenes would have wholeheartedly agreed whilst, at the same time, very directly contradicting the teaching of the Qumran Community Rule that you should hate your enemies.

2. Exclusive Dining

Contrary to other instructions in the Qumran Community Rule, Jesus is recorded as having accepted food from and eaten with people who were clearly **not** Essenes. In Luke 14, for example, He is said to have dined at the house of a prominent Pharisee and, according to Matthew 9, He was accused of eating with *"sinners and tax collectors"*.

He also contradicted a requirement in Community Rule 28 that the crippled, the lame and the blind should all be **excluded** from Community meals. They were presumably believed by those at Qumran (as they were by many in society) to have been cursed by God and therefore to be 'unclean'. It is inferred in John 9 that Jesus – in contrast to such thinking – challenged the belief that blindness is a curse from God, resulting from the person's sin or the sins of their parents. Indeed, once again pointedly contradicting the teaching of the Community Rule, He is quoted in Luke 14 as telling His host:

> *"When you give a banquet, **invite** the poor, the crippled, the lame and the blind and you will be blessed."*

3. Sabbath Healing

The Essenes had a strict attitude to Sabbath observance. Josephus' claim that they observed stricter practices than either the Sadducees or the Pharisees is confirmed by other writers and by the Dead Sea Scrolls. (Admittedly, however, the wording in the Scrolls regarding Sabbath rules is not always clear and even, on occasions, contradictory.)

The Gospels record that Jesus was criticised for healing people on the Sabbath Day. We are not told if His critics included Essenes, but it is certainly possible. He is quoted In Luke 2 as pointing out that *"the Sabbath was made for man and not man for the Sabbath"* and, in Matthew 12, as making the following case:

> *"If any of you has a sheep and it falls into a pit on the Sabbath, will you not take hold of it and lift it out? How much more valuable is a person than a sheep. Therefore,* **it is lawful to do good on the Sabbath.***"*

Interestingly, the issue of what to do about an animal which had stumbled into a pit on the Sabbath is specifically addressed in the Scrolls and in the traditions of the Pharisees (see Gemara Shabbos 128b). **Both** appear to agree that simply lifting it out of the pit on the Sabbath Day was unlawful. However, the question posed by Jesus would suggest that, in the **real** world, most people would have done just that!

4. Ritual Washing

The Pharisees ceremonially washed their hands before eating – a ritual going back to the instruction in Exodus 30 that priests must wash their hands and feet when presenting a food offering. The Essenes, according to Josephus, bathed completely before partaking in their communal meals.

Mark 7 recounts an occasion when a group of Pharisees noticed some of Jesus' disciples eating with unwashed hands and challenged Him about it. In response, He accused them of hypocrisy. But no claim is made in the Gospels that **Jesus Himself** failed to wash (or bathe) before meals or that He ever told others not to do so. And John 13 records that He washed the feet of His disciples at the Last Supper, telling the Apostle Peter:

> *"Those who have had a* **bath** *need only to wash their* ***feet***".

5. Public Preaching

Although some of the Essene groups living in other places were probably more open, the Qumran Community were an exclusive and inward-looking bunch. Jesus, in contrast, went around preaching to the Jewish people and is quoted in Matthew 5 as teaching:

> "*A town built on a hill cannot be hidden. Neither do people light a lamp and put it under a bowl. Instead, they put it on its stand, and it gives light to everyone in the house. In the same way let your light shine before others...*"

This quotation of Jesus is often used by Christians as an encouragement to be a witness to the light of the gospel. But the notion of lighting a lamp and then proceeding to place it under a bowl is one which is **laden with irony** (and perhaps even with a degree of sarcasm).

Jesus' words could easily have been interpreted by His listeners as reproving – or even as mocking – those who claimed to be '*the Sons of Light*' yet had failed to spread their message to others, instead staying closeted away at Qumran.

And I would suggest that four of Jesus' parables – 'the Parable of the Prodigal Son', 'the Parable of the Labourers', 'the Parable of the Unjust Steward' and 'the Parable of the Talents' – were also possibly intended as criticism of the Qumran leadership for their failure to engage in outreach.

Let us take some time to look at these interesting parables.

22. THE PRODIGAL'S BROTHER

The so-called '**Parable of the Prodigal Son**', recounted in Luke 15, is one I recall often hearing in my youth. Even as a child, it occurred to me that it is really a tale of **two sons** – one a prodigal, who squandered his inheritance but who then repented, and the other an obedient son, who remained at home faithfully working for his father.

Gospel preachers would make the point that, in the words of Isaiah 53:6, *"we all, like sheep, have gone astray"*. They would use the parable to illustrate the lesson that **we all** need to repent, to admit (as the prodigal did) *"I have sinned"* and *"am no longer worthy to be called your son"* and there is a loving heavenly Father who, like the earthly father in the parable, will welcome us.

But if this was the primary message of the parable (I remember thinking) why did Jesus introduce into the story the righteous elder son who resented the lavish reception laid on for his returning brother? Did doing so not only serve to confuse the lesson that we have **all** gone astray? And yet the **contrast** between these two brothers is clearly a central feature of the parable.

Indeed, Jesus made a similar contrast a little earlier in Luke 15, in the Parable of the Lost Sheep – one which has an obvious connection to the statement in Matthew 15:24 that He had been *"sent only to the lost sheep of Israel"*. In Luke 15:7, Jesus is quoted as saying there will be more rejoicing in heaven over a single sinner who repents ***"than over ninety-nine righteous people who do not need to repent."***

Essenes believed the kingdom of God was coming and that terrible judgement was soon to fall on Israel. Yet the Qumran Community had kept themselves pretty much to themselves. In contrast, Jesus actively preached to *"the lost sheep of Israel"*, warning that the kingdom of God was at hand, and urging people to repent.

The Parable of the Prodigal Son would not only have served to illustrate God's gracious forgiveness for the repenting sinner. It would also have challenged those – such as the Community at Qumran – who did not support Jesus' campaign of outreach to the lost.

Yes, these Essenes had forsaken worldly possessions and had righteously devoted themselves in quiet obedience to God. But, like the prodigal's brother, some may well have **resented** those of Jesus' converts who had lived sinful lives – squandering their inheritance as 'the sons of Abraham' – and who had repented only at the eleventh hour, as God's judgement (they believed) was about to fall upon the nation.

Just such resentment is addressed once again in the unusual **Parable of the Labourers** in Matthew 20. In this parable, labourers who worked in a vineyard from early morning grumbled about others who had been employed for only the last hour, yet who received the **same** reward at the end of the day. They were reminded that they had willingly agreed to a day's work for the wage they were given, and the master had every right to be generous to whomever he chose.

What then was the meaning of Jesus' Parable of the Labourers in Matthew 20, and how would it likely have been interpreted by His listeners? **Might not this parable have been another rebuke to the righteous 'Sons of Light' at Qumran and elsewhere who didn't support Jesus' campaign of outreach to sinners, and who were resentful of converts who had only come to repentance so late in the day?**

If so, it could also provide an explanation of Jesus' seemingly obscure Parable of the Unjust Steward, the one in which He is quoted as using the very term "*the sons of light*". It is this intriguing parable I would like us to consider next.

23. THE QUMRAN LEADERS AND THE UNJUST STEWARD

The problematic Parable of the Unjust Steward (or Dishonest Manager) is recounted in the first 12 verses of Luke 16. They read as follows:

> "There was a rich man whose manager was accused of wasting his possessions. So, he called him in and asked him, 'What is this I hear about you? Give an account of your management because you cannot be my manager any longer.' The manager said to himself, 'What shall I do now? My master is taking away my job. I'm not strong enough to dig and I'm ashamed to beg. I know what I'll do so that, when I lose my job here, people will welcome me into their houses.'
>
> So, he called in each one of his master's debtors. He asked the first, 'How much do you owe my master?' 'Nine hundred gallons of olive oil', he replied. The manager told him, 'Take your bill, sit down quickly and make it four hundred and fifty.' Then he asked the second, 'How much do you owe?' 'A thousand bushels of wheat', he replied. He told him, 'Take your bill and make it eight hundred.'
>
> **The master commended the dishonest manager because he had acted shrewdly, for the sons of this world are more shrewd in dealing with their own kind than are the people** [or sons] **of light. I tell you, use worldly wealth to gain friends for yourself so that, when it is gone, you will be welcomed into eternal dwellings.** Whoever can be trusted with very little can also be trusted with much and whoever is dishonest with very little will also be dishonest with much. So, if you have not been trustworthy in handling worldly wealth [or 'unrighteous mammon'], who will trust you with true riches. And if you have not been trustworthy with someone else's property, who will give you property of your own?"

This is acknowledged as being a genuine parable of Jesus by some of even the most sceptical of scholars, who regard it as much too obscure to have been invented by Christians.

Indeed, it has presented generations of Christians with difficulties because the manager is commended for his shrewdness in using the master's property to make friends. Many have debated the meaning of the parable, questioning how it can be reconciled with Christian values of honesty.

The parable begins with the statement that the manager had been accused of "*wasting*" his master's possessions. Some take this to imply he had **always** been dishonest or, at best, was **careless** in his management of the master's affairs.

However, you will note that **no** allegation of **previous** dishonesty is expressly made by Jesus. And, in addition, the way in which the manager was able to call in his master's debtors, who had each been given bills setting out what they owed, would suggest a reasonably **careful** standard of book-keeping on his part.

Could the accusation of him wasting his master's possessions therefore be referring to something else?

Both the "*wasting*" of which the manager was accused and him being "*commended*" for using the master's wealth to make friends could perhaps be explained if he had been employed, not to run a profit-making business (as we are inclined to assume), but instead for the purpose of benefiting others.

This was, of course, **precisely** the role of the Essene leaders, who acted as trustees (or **stewards**). Those joining the Essenes handed over their worldly possessions to the leaders to be used for the common good.

Josephus states that, although they despised personal wealth, the Essenes had many **collective** possessions.

Excavation at Qumran confirms that the group who lived there did indeed have substantial assets, including many coins (as documented by Father Roland de Vaux in his book *'Archaeology and the Dead Sea Scrolls'*). The fact these coins had not long since been stolen would suggest they had likely been hidden in the ground.

Some Essenes may well have felt the leaders at Qumran had been guilty of having **wasted** the resources entrusted to them by failing to use them to engage in a campaign of outreach to their fellow Jews.

Those *"lost sheep of Israel"* who, as a result of such outreach, repented and were saved from impending punishment would, in the afterlife, be there to welcome the leaders into their *"eternal dwellings"* in paradise.

Any Essenes who held such a view would have seen the parable as a criticism of those leaders.

This interpretation of the Parable of the Unjust Steward would then connect it to the much more well-known **Parable of the Talents** (or Bags of Gold) in Matthew 25.

In that parable, a man who was going on a journey entrusted his wealth to three of his servants. One of them was given five bags of gold, another three bags, and the third a single bag.

The first two servants used the gold to make a profit, but the servant who had been given only one bag simply buried it in the ground [in the same way the Qumran leaders had presumably done with money which had been entrusted to them].

Upon his eventual return, the master accused the third servant of being wicked and lazy, telling him:

> "*You should have put my money on deposit with the bankers so that, when I returned, I would have received it back with interest*" (Matthew 25:27).

Whilst also having a much wider application, Jesus' Parable of the Talents (like the Parable of the Unjust Steward) could have been a criticism of the Qumran leaders for **wasting** the Community's assets by failing to use them wisely to extend God's kingdom. Indeed, given their reluctance to engage in trade, they hadn't even earned any **interest** on the funds.

Such an interpretation would then link in well with the question raised by Jesus at the end of the Parable of the Unjust Steward:

> *"So, if you have not been trustworthy in handling **wordly** wealth, who will trust you with **true** riches?"*.

Some Essenes may have felt the Qumran leaders had wasted the earthly wealth – the 'unrighteous mammon' – given to them by others and couldn't therefore expect to be entrusted by God with "*true*" riches in a future age in a 'New Jerusalem'.

24. THE NEW TEMPLE AND THE NEW JERUSALEM

An important Qumran Scroll, which gives a revealing insight into Essene beliefs, is **the Temple Scroll**.

It contains a detailed blueprint for the construction of the Temple, sets out the rituals to be carried out in it and lists the various religious festivals to be held each year. These have several differences from the rituals and festivals which were observed by other Jews.

Essenes apparently believed the details contained in the Temple Scroll were given by God to Moses and had been passed down through the centuries to them. In their view, the Temple had not been built to the correct design and some of the practices carried out in it – such as the way in which animal sacrifices were conducted – were improper.

They held that terrible judgement was about to fall on Jerusalem, and the Second Temple (just like the First) would be completely destroyed – as indeed it was in 70AD.

We don't know if the Gospel of Mark was written before 70AD, but Mark 13:1-2 records that Jesus likewise predicted the destruction of the Second Temple buildings:

> As Jesus was leaving the temple one of his disciples said to him, "Look, Teacher! What massive stones! What magnificent buildings!"
>
> "Do you see all these great buildings?" replied Jesus, **"Not one stone will be left on another. Every stone will be thrown to the ground."**

Mark 13 quotes Him as going on to tell Peter, James, John and Andrew:

> "How dreadful it will be in those days for pregnant women and nursing mothers! Pray that this will not take place in winter,

because those will be days of distress unequalled from the beginning, when God created the world, until now – and never to be equalled again."

*"If the Lord had not cut short those days, no one would survive. **But for the sake of the Elect**, whom He has chosen, He will shorten them...."*

"In those days, following that distress, 'The sun will be darkened, and the moon will not give its light; the stars will fall from the sky and the heavenly bodies will be shaken'. At that time people will see the Son of Man coming in clouds with great power and glory. And He will send His angels and gather his elect from the four winds, from the ends of the earth to the ends of the heavens."

Essenes seemingly believed that, following God's coming judgement on Jerusalem and the destruction of the Temple, the Messiah would rebuild it according to what they held was the right design, as outlined in the Temple Scroll.

John 2:19-21 states that after clearing the Temple, driving out the animals, overturning the money changers' tables and scattering their coins, Jesus declared:

"Destroy this temple and I will raise it again in three days".

John goes on to provide the explanation that the temple of which Jesus was speaking was His own body and, after He had been raised from the dead, the disciples **then** recalled what He had said.

Surprisingly (but in common with many of the quotations of Jesus found in John) none of the other Gospels make any mention of this crucial statement.

According to Mark 14, however, when Jesus had been arrested and brought for trial before the Sanhedrin:

> *Then some stood up and gave this false testimony against him: "We heard him say, 'I will destroy this temple made with human hands and in three days will build another not made with hands'." Yet even then their testimony did not agree.*

And, in the following Chapter, Mark records that, as Jesus was subsequently being crucified, passers-by cruelly mocked Him, shouting:

> *"So, you who are going to destroy the Temple and build it in three days, come down from the cross and save yourself!"*

It would therefore appear that, whatever His disciples remembered of Jesus' words about raising the Temple, some of the Jewish people were aware of the allegation He had said He would destroy the Temple and rebuild it in three days.

Essenes saw themselves as guardians of the truth about the correct dimensions and rituals for the Temple until the coming day of God's judgement upon Jerusalem.

They believed that, following the Temple's destruction, the Messiah would rebuild it according to the plan set out in the Temple Scroll. This, they held, would usher in a new age when, under a *"New Covenant"*, they (as God's *"Elect"*) would assume the priestly duties of the Temple in a *"New Jerusalem"*.

The term *"New Covenant"* – which of course occurs several times in the New Testament – is used in the Dead Sea Scrolls (in Damascus Document 9) and comes from Jeremiah 31:31.

The term *"the Elect"* is also used in the Scrolls and is found in the New Testament, such as in the words of Jesus in Mark 13 (*"But for the sake of the Elect..."*) quoted above.

As for the term *"New Jerusalem"*, it is not expressly used in the Old Testament but is nevertheless found in 11 Qumran Scrolls 18 (11Q18). Interestingly, it is also used in Revelation 3:12 & 21:9.

Until such times as the destruction and rebuilding of the Temple and the establishment by God of this 'New Jerusalem', it is evident from the contents of Damascus Document 8 that those Essenes living in the Judean desert at Qumran identified themselves with the following words found in Isaiah 40:

> *...a voice of one calling in the wilderness, "Prepare the way of the Lord, make straight in the desert a highway for our God"*.

25. BAPTISM, LOCUSTS AND WILD HONEY

It is hardly surprising that many people have associated the Essenes with John the Baptist, about whom Matthew 3 records the following:

> *In those days John the Baptist came preaching in the wilderness of Judea and saying, "Repent for the kingdom of heaven has come near". This is he who was spoken of through the prophet Isaiah: "A voice of one calling in the wilderness, 'Prepare the way of the Lord, make straight paths for him'".*
>
> *John's clothes were made of camel's hair, and he had a leather belt around his waist. His food was locusts and wild honey. People went out to him from Jerusalem and all Judea and the whole region of the Jordan. Confessing their sins, they were baptised by him in the River Jordan.*

According to Matthew, therefore, John preached in the Judean desert, near the River Jordan – in other words, not far from Qumran.

In common with Mark and Luke, Matthew identifies John with the voice referred to in Isaiah 40, calling in the wilderness, "*Prepare the way of the Lord*". As we've seen, this was the very same description with which the Qumran Essenes associated themselves. And He is depicted in the first Chapter of John's Gospel as having been *"a witness to the light"* – another term with which Essenes would have readily identified.

Although (in Antiquities 18) Josephus writes at some length about John the Baptist, he does not mention there being any link between John and the Essenes. He **also** doesn't mention any connection between John and Jesus. Much of his account, however, accords with those in the New Testament Gospels. He confirms that John was a good man who preached of the need to repent and live righteously, crowds came to hear him, and many were baptised.

Like the Gospels, Josephus records that John was put to death by Herod Antipas, who the Gospels simply refer to as *"Herod"*. He claims (in Antiquities 18.116) that some people believed a military defeat subsequently suffered by Herod Antipas was a punishment from God for his unjust killing of John. Mark's Gospel explains that John had angered Herod [Antipas] by criticising him for having married Herodias, the ex-wife of his brother Philip.

In Jewish Law, Leviticus 20 renders it unlawful for a man to marry certain relatives, including his brother's former wife and his aunt. The Essenes went further still – Damascus Document 5.11 declares it to be wrong for a man to marry **his niece**. Now Herodias was the granddaughter of King Herod and was thus a niece of Herod Antipas.

To Essenes, the marriage of Herodias to Herod Antipas was very wrong. Not only had she previously been married to his brother, but she was also his niece. And on top of that (according to Josephus) they had fallen in love when they were married to others and had each divorced in order to wed. As we've seen, the Essenes were opposed to divorce. **To say that Essenes would not have approved of the union would therefore be something of an understatement!**

John the Baptist's outspoken criticism of the marriage – about which he clearly felt strongly, and which sadly cost him his life – reflected the Essene view that it was an abomination in the sight of God for Herod Antipas to have married his divorced niece Herodias.

Mark 6 relates the story of John's execution. Herod Antipas is said to have been so delighted by a dance performed by his stepdaughter at his birthday party, he rashly offered to give her anything she wanted. Prompted by her mother Herodias, who held a grudge against John for denouncing her marriage, she asked for the head of John the Baptist on a platter. Although having a respect for John [as he seemingly also did for the Essenes, who he believed could predict the future], Herod Antipas granted her request and John was beheaded.

Whilst Josephus records that John was executed by Herod Antipas, he makes no mention of the extraordinary incident of the birthday party described in Matthew and Mark. Neither does he say John was related to Jesus, as is recorded in the Gospel of Luke.

And Josephus does not refer to John speaking of Jesus as being someone greater, who would come after him and who would "*baptise with the Holy Spirit*", as is stated in Mark 1. However, it seems from what is said in Luke 7, that this was something about which John himself was not always entirely sure:

> *News about Jesus spread throughout Judea and the surrounding country. John's disciples told him about these things. Calling two of them, he sent them to the Lord to ask him,* "**Are you the one who is to come, or should we expect someone else?**"

Acts 19 tells of a later encounter between the Apostle Paul and some disciples of John the Baptist. When Paul asked them if they had received the Holy Spirit, they replied, *"No, we have not even heard **that there is a Holy Spirit**".* It would therefore appear that not only Josephus but also some of John's own disciples were unaware of him speaking of a coming One who would baptise with the Holy Spirit – or indeed of him having ever even mentioned the Holy Spirit.

According to Acts, these disciples of John became Christians. Other disciples of John likely became followers of Jesus, especially after John's execution. And, although it is indicated in Luke 7 that Jesus and His disciples differed in their practices from John by **eating bread** and **drinking wine** (which John evidently did **not** do), Jesus' initial teachings appear to have been much **the same** as those of John.

Essenes believed God's judgement was about to fall upon the nation and on the corrupt Temple regime in Jerusalem. This, they held, would lead to the establishment by God of a **new** Temple and the coming of the kingdom of heaven. Did John the Baptist, I wonder, share a similar expectation?

Well, from what is recorded in Matthew 3, John's message would appear to have included the following five main themes:

1. The kingdom of heaven was close at hand. (Jesus is likewise quoted as speaking of the kingdom of heaven, declaring that it was near.)

2. God's wrath was soon to be displayed in judgement on the unrighteous. The pictures said to have been used by John are of an axe already placed at the base of trees which did not produce good fruit and of chaff which would be burned with unquenchable fire. (Jesus is documented as similarly warning of God's judgement, employing the same imagery as that used by John.)

3. His listeners should repent and turn to God. (Jesus is quoted in Matthew 4:17 as preaching the same message: *"Repent of your sins and turn to God, for the kingdom of heaven is near"*.)

4. Having repented, they should be baptised. John's baptism, it would seem, was not dissimilar to the initiation ritual of the Essenes. (According to the Gospels, Jesus' disciples likewise baptised converts and Jesus was Himself baptised by John.)

5. They should live righteous lives in keeping with genuine repentance and should share their possessions with those in need. In similarity with the Essenes, John is recorded in Luke 3:11 as specifically advocating the sharing of **food and clothing**. (As we noted earlier, the same theme is addressed by Jesus in the Sermon on the Mount.)

So, we can see that all the recorded teachings of John the Baptist reflected the beliefs of the Essenes and are repeated in the teachings of Jesus.

And Jesus is quoted as using some of the **very same terms** as John, such as *"kingdom of heaven"* (Matthew 3:2 & 4:17), *"good fruit"* and *"cut down and thrown into the fire"* (Matthew 3:10 & 7:19) and *"brood of vipers"* (Matthew 3:8 & 23:33). Given that we don't have many quotations of John the Baptist, **it is reasonably likely that some more of the teachings**

of Jesus had also previously been those of John. It is not beyond the bounds of possibility, for example, that parts of the Sermon on the Mount had first been preached by John, or by others (such as, perhaps, Essenes).

Luke (alone) records that Jesus and John were related through their respective mothers, Mary and Elizabeth. Whilst some scholars treat Luke's claim with scepticism, the historical and theological links between Jesus and John are not easily denied.

In fact, following John's execution, some of the Jewish people – with their superstitions and all their talk of resurrection – seemingly thought Jesus **was** John the Baptist raised from the dead (see Mark 6:14).

The Gospels record that, following His baptism by John, Jesus was led into the desert – presumably the Judean wilderness around Qumran – where He was tempted by the Devil. Mark 4:11 says He received ministry from "*angels*" ("*messengers*"). Some have suggested this may be a reference to the white-clothed Essenes of Qumran, but there is little or no evidence to support their theory.

It is nevertheless noteworthy that the Qumran Community lived near to where John baptised and likewise had an initiation ritual which involved immersion in water. And, in precisely the same way as with John, they were identified with the prophesy of a voice crying in the wilderness of Judea, "*Prepare the way of the Lord!*".

Despite the striking similarities, the most obvious **difference** between John the Baptist and the Qumran Essenes was that, whilst they did not mix much with outsiders, John made a point of preaching to the public and actively seeking converts. According to Luke 1:80, however, John "***lived in the wilderness until he appeared publicly to Israel***".

It is therefore quite possible John was a **former** member of the Qumran Community who had left or been expelled – perhaps as a result of disagreeing with them about the need to go public with their message of God's coming judgement upon the nation.

Community Rule 5.15 instructed members of the Community not to eat any food which came from outsiders. As we saw previously, Josephus claims that Essenes swore not to do so. Those who were expelled yet who wished to abide by their oaths, he says, were unable to accept supplies from non-Essenes and had to find their own food from the land.

If John the Baptist was indeed a former member of the Qumran Community, then, to remain true to his solemn vows, he would not have been able to accept food from others. He could only eat what he himself was able to obtain in the desert. This would then provide a decidedly plausible explanation for the reference in Luke 7:33 to him not eating bread and that in Matthew 3:4 to his unusual diet of locusts and wild honey.

Locusts are one of the few insects regarded in Jewish Law as 'clean' and lawful to eat. They are also, I'm told, an excellent source of protein and are mentioned as food in some of the Qumran Scrolls. And if the Essene rule applied to clothes as well as to food – which seems logical – this might also explain John's camel hair clothing.

26. THE CLEARING OF THE TEMPLE

In the Book *'Every Good Man is Free'*, the first century historian Philo of Alexandria claims that Essenes showed their devotion to God:

> "... **not** by offering animal sacrifices, but by resolving to render **their minds** truly holy".

Many scholars nevertheless think it probable that Essenes did sacrifice animals, for which (according to Josephus in Antiquities 18.1.5) they had their own unique rituals. It may therefore be the case that it was just **some** Essene groups who didn't offer animal sacrifices; or perhaps Philo was referring to the emphasis placed by Essenes upon the centrality of **purity of heart**, or mind.

Whether or not Essenes at the time of Jesus sacrificed animals, however, it is evident they were vehemently opposed to the **Temple regime**, to its ways of conducting sacrifices and to the role played by **money changers**. The Temple courts had money changers who would – no doubt at a hefty profit – exchange Roman and other coins for Tyrian shekels. Having a high silver content, Tyrian shekels were the only coins accepted **inside** the Temple to buy animals for sacrifice.

As mentioned previously, some Essenes seemingly did not engage in trade or use Roman coins (other, presumably, than to pay taxes to Rome). Roman coins not only contained less silver but were considered by some Jews to be in breach of the Ten Commandments, having on them 'graven images' of the heads of the Caesars, who were regarded as gods.

Being firmly opposed to any form of commercialism, Essenes would have been totally outraged by a Temple system they believed was not following the correct rituals for sacrifices, was profaning the House of God by trading in the Temple courts using money with graven images, and (to top it all) was engaging in profiteering!

Jesus, according to the Gospels, forcibly cleared the Temple, overturning the tables of the money changers, driving out the traders and condemning the Temple regime as being nothing less than "*a den of robbers*".

The clearance of the Temple is recorded in Matthew 21, in Mark 11 & in Luke 19 as happening near the **end** of Jesus' public ministry and shortly before His arrest and crucifixion. In John's Gospel, however, it is described in Chapter 2 as occurring **early** in His ministry. Although each of the Gospels refer to just one such episode, some Christians feel there must have been **two** separate incidents. Others think this highly unlikely.

We don't of course know if Jesus cleared the Temple more than once, however unlikely it may seem. But, as with John the Baptist's criticism of the marriage of Herod Antipas, **there can be little doubt that Jesus' dramatic actions and denunciation of the Temple system mirrored the sense of outrage felt towards it by the Essenes.**

According to Mark 11:18, it was after the clearance of the Temple by Jesus that the Jewish chief priests began looking for a way to have Him killed. It is striking, therefore, that the executions of both Jesus and John the Baptist appear to have resulted from words and actions which matched the views held by Essenes (regarding, in the case of John, the marriage of Herod Antipas to Herodias, and in that of Jesus, the corrupt nature of the Temple regime).

27. ENOCH AND THE CALENDAR

Another fascinating fact I was to learn about the Essenes is that **they used a different calendar from everyone else**. Their Calendar is referred to in various of the Qumran Scrolls and is outlined in the Book of 1 Enoch. It was supposedly given by the archangel Uriel to the Old Testament character Enoch (the great-grandfather of Noah) who is said in Genesis 5 to have lived for all of **365** years.

The Calendar year had four seasons, each comprising exactly 13 weeks. The seasons consisted of three months, two of the months having 30 days and the other 31 days. There were therefore 91 days in each of the four seasons and **364** days in a year.

The problem with using a calendar which has only 364 days in a year is that, over time, the seasons would of course get out of order! Being sophisticated students of the skies, however, it is most unlikely the Essenes did not realise that – as with the number of Enoch's alleged years of life – there are **365** (and a bit) days in a year. So, it's likely that every seventh year an extra week was added and observed as a week of rest. (Interestingly, if a further week was added every 49th year and another in each 70th year – Essenes having seemingly been somewhat obsessed with using the number seven – the result would be an almost perfect fit with 70 true years.)

One of the differences with John's Gospel is that it has the Last Supper occurring on the night before Passover (Wednesday). Matthew, Mark & Luke, on the other hand, each indicate it was held on the **following** night (Thursday). Most Bible commentators agree there is a discrepancy between the Gospel accounts, but few solutions have been found which could harmonise them. (Whilst there might perhaps have been two clearances of the Temple, there obviously can't have been two Last Suppers!) **A possible explanation for the difference is that the writer of John's Gospel may have been using the Essene's Calendar.**

It is thought by some archaeologists (such as Bargil Pixner, a Benedictine monk who has excavated extensively in the area) that the place believed from early times to be the site of the Last Supper was in the Essene Quarter of Jerusalem. It is close to a gate they think is the one referred to by Josephus in Jewish Wars 5 as *"the Gate of the Essenes"*. This then raises the possibility that **Jesus Himself** used the Essene's Calendar. Indeed, none less than the late Pope Benedict, in an Easter sermon he gave in 2007 (number 20070405), acknowledged that this may perhaps account for the difference between the date of the Last Supper in John and that in Matthew, Mark & Luke.

A Bible verse which might **also** point to the Last Supper having been held in the Essene Quarter of Jerusalem is Luke 22:10, in which the disciples sent by Jesus to prepare for it (Peter and John) were told to follow *"a **man** carrying a jar of water"*. This was a most unusual sight. As is still the case in many African countries today, carrying water was firmly regarded as being **women's** work. Men who lived in celibate Essene communities, however, had to carry out such tasks for themselves. The man with the jar of water, therefore, may well have been an Essene.

There is no record of which I am aware of Jesus ever using the Essene's Calendar. But whether He did or not, there appears to be the possibility of some sort of link between Jesus and the Essenes which cannot be lightly dismissed. And, as I will attempt to outline in the next few chapters, I discovered some remarkable connections between 1 Enoch (the book which describes the Calendar) and certain passages in the Bible. To my amazement, these were some of the same Bible passages I referred to in Chapter 1, and which had puzzled me for years!

28. THE BOOK OF 1 ENOCH

1 Enoch is an interesting book, if also a rather peculiar one. As with the Old Testament Book of Daniel, another favourite of the Essenes, it is thought by scholars to be a collection of the writings of various authors, written at different times.

Amazingly, some parts of 1 Enoch might possibly have been written more than three centuries before the birth of Jesus. The most recent parts – Chapters 37-71 (which are collectively known as '*the Book of Parables*') and Chapter 108 – could have been penned anywhere between 150BC and 150AD. An important fact to keep in mind is that it is **only the older** chapters of 1 Enoch which have been discovered in the Dead Sea Scrolls.

Very few people today believe any of 1 Enoch to be the work of Enoch, the man said in Genesis 5 to be from the **seventh** generation of mankind. Genesis states that, during his 365 years on earth, Enoch "*walked faithfully with God*" before God "*took him away*" and he "*was no more*". Very little else is said in the Bible about Enoch, but Hebrews 11:5 claims he did not experience death and was taken (or, as some versions have it, "*translated*") directly to heaven. Enoch was evidently revered by early Christians, who would seem to have believed he existed and wrote at least part of the Book.

1 Enoch is an eclectic mix of writings. One section sets out the 364-day Calendar, whilst others are narrative. Some parts detail the movements of the planets, and others name and describe angels. Meanwhile, Chapters 83-90 (which, although not found at Qumran, are thought to have been written over a century before Christ) relate visions much like those described in the Book of Revelation.

Today, only the scriptures of the Ethiopian Coptic Church (one of the Eastern Orthodox Churches) and *Beta Israel* (the African Jews) contain 1 Enoch. But it was widely read by early Christians. It is referred to in various Christian books written prior to the compiling of the New Testament (which wasn't put together in its present form until the end of the fourth century).

Tertullian, a second century church leader and an architect of the doctrine of the Trinity, speaks highly of Enoch, calling it "*the **scripture** of Enoch*" (in his book *'On the Apparel of Women'*). The Church Father Clement of Alexandria (in *'Ecologue'* 2.1) similarly talks of it as "*scripture*". And the renowned Christian scholar Origen (in *'De Principiis'* Book 4) appears to have regarded it as having the same authority as the Old Testament Psalms.

Many Christians today simply ignore 1 Enoch, some even considering it heretical. Yet the New Testament Letter of **Jude** (which, as with James, may possibly have been written by a brother of Jesus) has strong connections with 1 Enoch. Although comprising just 25 verses, Jude refers not only to "*stars*" and to "*celestial beings*" but also to "*angels*". As we've seen, stars and angels were of great importance to Essenes. Jude also talks about "*the archangel Michael*", someone who is frequently mentioned in the Qumran Scrolls.

What is more (as we shall now see) Jude even goes so far as to quote from 1 Enoch!

29. HEY, JUDE!

Verse 9 of the first Chapter **1 Enoch** reads as follows:

> *And behold He is coming with ten thousand of His holy ones to execute judgement upon everyone and to destroy all the ungodly; and to convict all flesh of all the works of ungodliness which they have committed and of all the harsh things which ungodly sinners have spoken against Him.*

Now here are verses 14 & 15 from the Book of **Jude**:

> **Enoch**, *the seventh from Adam,* **prophesied** *about these men: "See, the Lord is coming with thousands upon thousands of his holy ones to judge everyone and to convict all the ungodly of all the ungodly acts they have done in an ungodly way, and of all the harsh words ungodly sinners have spoken against him."*

There can surely be no question these verses in Jude are taken from 1 Enoch. The writer clearly states that the words he quotes are those of *"Enoch, the seventh from Adam"* – the person referred to in Genesis 5.

Indeed, the term *"seventh from Adam"* is used in 1 Enoch itself (in 1 Enoch 60.8) and would seem – given the significance which was attributed to the number seven – to emphasise Enoch's importance.

And not only does the writer of Jude quote from 1 Enoch but claims (in verse 14) that Enoch *"prophesied"*, asserting that the quotation from Enoch is prophecy.

Christians who believe each word in Jude to have been dictated to the writer by the Holy Spirit point out that, simply because a verse from 1 Enoch is quoted in it, does not of course mean the Book of 1 Enoch is itself divinely inspired. But they are nevertheless left with the following inevitable conclusions:

1. The words contained in 1 Enoch and quoted in verses 14 & 15 of Jude **were** either written or spoken by the Old Testament character Enoch.

2. The whole of the Book of 1 Enoch cannot be ignored but contains genuine words of Enoch, words which constitute **prophecy** – that is, words given by God to Enoch which have the same authority as those of the Old Testament Prophets.

3. The prophetic words of Enoch quoted in Jude can only have found their way **into the Book of 1 Enoch** in one of the following ways:

    (a) at least some of 1 Enoch **was** written by Enoch himself, **or**

    (b) God directly revealed to **the writer of 1 Enoch 1** words which had been spoken or written by Enoch, **or**

    (c) valid writings (or oral traditions) were passed down through the centuries from the time of Enoch to the writer of 1 Enoch 1.

For those who don't regard Jude as infallible, on the other hand, the solution is a simple one – namely, that the writer of Jude thought 1 Enoch contained prophecy written by Enoch and therefore quoted from it.

30. 'THE NEPHILIM' AND THE SPIRITS IN PRISON

Chapters 6-11 of 1 Enoch (which, like Chapter 1, are contained in the Dead Sea Scrolls) expand upon the following verses at the start of **Genesis 6**, immediately before the story of **Noah** and the ark:

> *When human beings began to increase in number on the earth and daughters were born to them,* **the sons of God** *saw that the daughters of humans were beautiful, and they married any of them they chose. Then the Lord said, "My spirit will not contend with humans for ever, for they are mortal. Their days will be 120 years".*
>
> **The Nephilim** *were on the earth in those days – and afterwards – when the sons of God went to the daughters of humans and had children by them. They were the heroes of old, men of renown.*

Unsurprisingly, these unusual Bible verses, to which I referred in Chapter 1, have been a source of debate for centuries. Generations of Christians have asked the questions: Just who were *"the sons of God"* said to have married *"the daughters of humans"*; and who or what were *"the Nephilim"*?

The Nephilim (whose name, I gather, means *"***those who have fallen***"*) crop up again later in the Old Testament. Numbers 13 records that spies sent by Moses to check out the land of Canaan reported back:

> *"All the people we saw there are of great size. We saw the Nephilim there (the descendants of Anak come from the Nephilim). We seemed like grasshoppers…"*

It would seem the *Nephilim* were regarded by Jewish people as having been fearsome giants of old.

As for the term "***the sons of God***", it is widely agreed that, when used in the Book of Job, it refers to **angels**. Some think it has the **same** meaning when used in above passage in Genesis 6.

Others, however, contend that in Genesis the term *"the sons of God"* instead refers to **men** (in a similar way in which the first man Adam is described in Luke 3:38 as *"the son of God"*) and the writer is simply saying, in effect, that men married women and had children.

1 Enoch elaborates on the story told in Genesis 6, claiming that the sons of God referred to were two hundred fallen angels who left heaven, came to earth and married women. It lists the names of their leaders and outlines the skills they each brought to earth. It also describes the sinfulness of their children, alleging **this** to be the reason why God sent the Flood in the days of Noah. **According to 1 Enoch, it is the offspring of the fallen angels and their human partners who were the *Nephilim* – *"those who have fallen"*.**

Talk of angels abandoning heaven, coming to earth and taking human wives might seem to us quite bizarre. (I, myself, don't know any women who claim to be married to angels – not even fallen ones!)

But such an event may also be alluded to in three New Testament books. Let me try to explain.

In **1 Peter 3:19**, Christ is said to have gone and preached (or made a proclamation) to *"**the imprisoned spirits**"*. Within the context of the Bible alone, the term *"the imprisoned spirits"* has no clearly obvious meaning. For countless years this verse has (in the words of the sixteenth century theologian John Calvin) *"puzzled many minds"*.

The spirits in prison are described in 1 Peter as being *"those who were disobedient long ago, when God waited in the days of **Noah**"*. The word *"spirits"* could perhaps refer to **angels** (as is the case in Hebrews 1, where the writer asks, *"Are not all angels ministering spirits?"*). Then in **2 Peter 2:4** it says:

> *If God did not spare angels when they sinned but sent them to hell, putting them in chains of darkness to be held for judgement and if He did not spare the ancient world when He brought the flood on its ungodly people, but protected Noah...*

So, 1 Peter speaks of *"spirits"* in prison who were disobedient in the days of Noah. And 2 Peter (which likewise goes on to talk about Noah) states that God did not spare *"angels when they sinned"* but put them in chains of darkness.

Neither of these references obviously relate to any events described in the Old Testament. But they could possibly be referring to the story in 1 Enoch of disobedient angels who left heaven and came to earth before the Flood.

Meanwhile, **verses 6-11 of Jude** say this:

> *And **the angels who did not keep their positions of authority but abandoned their proper dwelling – these He has kept in darkness, bound with everlasting chains for judgement on that great Day**. In a similar way, Sodom and Gomorrah and the surrounding towns gave themselves up to sexual immorality and perversion. They serve as an example of those who suffer the punishment of eternal fire.*
>
> *In the very same way, on the strength of their dreams these ungodly people pollute their own bodies, reject authority and heap abuse on celestial beings. But even the archangel Michael, when he was disputing with the Devil about the body of Moses, did not himself dare to condemn him for slander but said, "The Lord rebuke you!" Yet these people slander whatever they do not understand and the very things they do understand by instinct – as irrational animals do – will destroy them. Woe to them! They have taken the way of Cain; they have rushed for profit into Balaam's error; they have been destroyed in Korah's rebellion.*

There are several strange references in these verses from Jude, the most intriguing being to a dispute between the archangel Michael and the Devil about the body of Moses. **No** such a dispute is mentioned in **any** previous writings of which I am aware. So, from where then does this reference come?

Some Christians claim the dispute between Michael and the Devil was something revealed directly by God **only** to the writer of Jude. But what, you might well ask, would have been the point in God giving to Jude the example of an event which no one knew about? Many scholars think it more likely Jude is referring to an account contained in some ancient book, read by early Christians, but which has long since been lost.

What is much more relevant to the story in 1 Enoch of disobedient angels leaving heaven, however, is Jude's talk of "*the angels who did not keep their positions of authority but who abandoned their proper dwelling*". **This has striking similarities to the reference in 2 Peter 2:4 to angels who sinned. But once again, no such angels are described anywhere in the Old Testament.**

Given that (as we've seen) Jude goes on to quote from 1 Enoch just a couple of verses later, might not Jude likely also be referring to the story in 1 Enoch of angels who sinned by abandoning heaven, coming to earth and marrying human wives?

31. FALLEN ANGELS AND 'THE ABYSS'

Angels, I gather, are only ever referred to in the Bible using the masculine form of the word. According to Mark 12:25, Jesus said:

> "When the dead rise, they will neither marry nor be given in marriage; they will be like the angels in heaven".

Some take this statement to mean that **no** angels could ever have married women.

But these words in Mark regarding *"the angels in heaven"* do **not** in fact contradict the claim made in 1 Enoch that there were disobedient angels who **left heaven**, came to earth and took human wives. Indeed, it could even be argued that the link made between the angels *"in heaven"* (as opposed to those angels who are no longer in heaven) and the subject of **marriage** is yet another **similarity** with 1 Enoch.

Jude says the angels who abandoned their positions of authority are now:

> "... kept in darkness, **bound with everlasting chains for judgement on the great Day**" (Jude verse 6).

Once again, I'm not aware of any reference in the Old Testament to angels who have been bound in chains and are awaiting judgement.

1 Enoch, however, **does** claim that God told the archangel Michael to bind the angels who had sinned by abandoning heaven, coming to earth and taking human wives. According to 1 Enoch 10.12, Michael was instructed to "*bind them fast... until the Day of their judgement*".

So, to summarise, not only does the writer of Jude quote directly from 1 Enoch, not only does he refer to angels who left their *"proper dwelling"*, but he also says these angels were bound in chains until the Day of their judgement – just as is described in 1 Enoch.

And the connections between 1 Enoch and the New Testament don't end there! Chapter 54 of 1 Enoch (which, admittedly, was not found at Qumran) claims the fallen angels will, on the Day of Judgement, be thrown into "**the Abyss of Fire**". There aren't any references to "*the Abyss*" in the Old Testament, yet the term occurs no less than seven times in the Book of Revelation.

Interestingly, it is also used in Luke 8, which describes the exorcism by Jesus of a demon-possessed man. Verses 31-32 say the demons begged Jesus not to order them to go "***into the Abyss***" and He gave them permission to enter a herd of pigs. The concept of demons being sent to an Abyss is not an express part of Old Testament theology. But it does, on the other hand, fit with that of 1 Enoch, in which there **are** said to be demons who will be consigned to the Abyss – although **not until** the Day of their judgement. (Indeed, might this perhaps explain why Jesus did not send the demons to the Abyss but allowed them to go into the pigs? The granting of this request by Jesus is something I had always found surprising.)

Yet again, the above references in Jude and in Luke appear to me to have much more in common with 1 Enoch than they do with any of the books of the Old Testament.

32. JUDE, 2 PETER AND 'CELESTIAL BEINGS'

Given the number of strange references found in the short Letter of Jude, some Christians (such as Martin Luther) have argued that it should not be included with the other books of the Bible.

In the fourth century – before the compilation of the New Testament as we have it today – there was indeed some debate as to whether or not Jude should be included.

It is one of twelve books which, although widely read in Christian churches, were listed as being "***disputed***".

Also in this list were books known as 'the Acts of Paul', 'the Letter of Barnabas', 'the Revelation of Peter', 'the Shepherd of Hermas' and 'the *Didache'* (or 'Teachings of the Twelve Apostles') – none of which, in the end, made it into the Bible.

But the list of disputed books also included Hebrews, James, 2 Peter, 2 & 3 John and Revelation – which of course (like Jude) **were** all eventually included in what we now know as the New Testament. Of these books, the most controversial was possibly Revelation, the authorship and contents of which were regarded with scepticism by many.

Even though the brief Letter of Jude might well have been written by a brother of Jesus, it must surely have been tempting to leave it out of the New Testament. Christianity would have lost little by its exclusion, whilst the quotation from 1 Enoch and the other problematic references in it could have been neatly side-stepped.

However, getting rid of inconvenient references in the Book of Jude is not quite such a simple matter! The contents of Jude bear striking similarities to a section of 2 Peter, and it would not be easy to justify rejecting Jude without also rejecting 2 Peter.

Here, once again, are verses 6-10 of **Jude**:

> And the angels who did not keep their positions of authority but abandoned their proper dwelling – these He has kept in darkness, **bound with everlasting chains for judgement** on that great Day. In a similar way, **Sodom and Gomorrah** and the surrounding towns gave themselves up to sexual immorality and perversion. They serve as an example of those who suffer the punishment of eternal fire.
>
> In the very same way, on the strength of their dreams these ungodly people pollute their own bodies, **reject authority and heap abuse on celestial beings**. But even the archangel Michael, when he was disputing with the Devil about the body of Moses, did not himself dare to condemn him for slander but said, "The Lord rebuke you!" Yet these people slander whatever they do not understand and the very things they do understand by instinct – **as irrational animals do** – will destroy them.

Compare those words in Jude with the following extracts taken from the 2nd Chapter of **2 Peter**:

> For if God did not spare angels when they sinned, but sent them to hell, **putting them in chains of darkness to be held for judgement**. If He did not spare the ancient world when He brought the flood... if He condemned the cities of **Sodom and Gomorrah** by burning them... then the Lord knows how to hold the unrighteous for punishment on the day of judgement.
>
> This is especially true of those who follow the corrupt desire of the flesh and **despise authority**. Bold and arrogant, they are not afraid to **heap abuse on celestial beings**. Yet **even angels**, although they are stronger and more powerful, do not heap abuse upon such beings when bringing judgement on them from the Lord. But these people blaspheme in matters they do not understand. They are **like unreasoning animals**...

You will note that, in the same way as in Jude, 2 Peter speaks of angels who sinned and who have been bound in chains awaiting judgement. (As we've already seen, this is something which, although not mentioned in the Old Testament, is described in 1 Enoch.)

Again, just like Jude, 2 Peter refers to God's judgement on the cities of Sodom and Gomorrah (the story of which is told in the Old Testament, in Genesis 19).

And then, using some identical wording to Jude, 2 Peter condemns those who, like *"unreasoning animals"*, arrogantly reject authority and *"heap abuse on celestial beings"*.

So, who or what (you may likely ask) **are the *"celestial beings"* to whom Jude and 2 Peter refer?** This particular term – translated in some versions as *"**dignities**"* – is not used elsewhere in the Bible.

Once again, there would seem to be a good deal of confusion among Christian commentators (or at least among those unfamiliar with 1 Enoch) as to what the term means. Some suggest the *"celestial beings"* are simply the angels. But that doesn't fit with 2 Peter 2, which states (in verse 11) that *"**even angels**"*, although stronger, don't heap abuse on them.

A possible clue to the meaning can perhaps be found in the Greek term which is used in 2 Peter 2:4 and translated (in the New International Version) as *"sent them to hell"*. I gather that the literal translation of this Greek term is *"cast them into Tartarus"* – another term not found anywhere else in the Bible.

Surprisingly, the word *"Tartarus"* comes from Greek mythology. It was the name given by Greeks to a place where the wicked were believed to receive divine punishment.

But, whilst not used elsewhere in the Bible, the name *"Tartarus"* is (yet again) **one which is found in the Book of 1 Enoch**. It occurs in none other than Chapter 20, the chapter of 1 Enoch which lists the names the **seven archangels**:

> *... and these are the names of the holy angels who watch:* **Uriel**, *one of the holy angels, who is over the world and over* **Tartarus**...
> (1 Enoch 20.2).

Given that Jude quotes from 1 Enoch and that 2 Peter uses the term *"cast them into Tartarus"* – a place mentioned in the very chapter of 1 Enoch which names the archangels – might not the *"celestial beings"* referred to in Jude and in 2 Peter likely be the disobedient archangels described in 1 Enoch?

Indeed, the condemnation of those who *"heap abuse"* on celestial beings could perhaps link in once more with the notion of the sun, the moon and the planets **being archangels**. You will recall that Josephus claims the sun was treated with reverence by Essenes, who are said by him to have covered themselves from its rays when going to the toilet. Those who refused to do likewise would presumably have been regarded by Essenes as arrogantly rejecting authority and as showing disrespect to (or 'heaping abuse on') celestial beings.

33. 1 ENOCH AND THE BOOK OF REVELATION

Not only does 1 Enoch have strong connections to the Letters of Jude and 2 Peter, but it also has many similarities with the Book of Revelation.

I have already alluded to the reference made in Revelation 8 to seven angels who stand before God and that in Revelation 12 to the fall of Satan and his angels to earth. Both feature in 1 Enoch, but not in the Old Testament.

Then, following the description of a huge red dragon which swept a third of the stars out of the sky and flung them to the earth, Revelation 12 continues:

> ...war broke out in heaven. **Michael and his angels** fought against the dragon, and the dragon and his angels fought back. But he was not strong enough and they lost their place in heaven. The great dragon was hurled down – that ancient serpent called the devil, or Satan, who leads the whole world astray. He was hurled to the earth and his angels with him...

The reference here to Michael, who with his angels fought against the dragon, is presumably to the **archangel** Michael.

As we've already seen, the archangel Michael is mentioned in Jude. He also features prominently in 1 Enoch, and in others of the Qumran Scrolls, where – as in Revelation – he is a leader of angels.

The contents of Revelation have a great deal in common, both in their wording and in their style, with the sections of 1 Enoch which recount visions. Take, for example, the following extracts taken from Chapters 71, 46 & 47 of 1 Enoch (which, I should point out, are all in the section known as *'the Book of Parables'* and have not been found in any of the Dead Sea Scrolls):

> *My spirit was translated and **I ascended into the heavens** and saw the holy sons of God. They were stepping on flames of fire. Their garments were white and their faces shone like snow… and I saw there a structure built of crystals and between those crystals tongues of living fire… and I saw angels who could not be counted – a thousand thousands and ten thousand times ten thousand encircling the house… and with them the Head of Days, his head white and pure as wool and his raiment indescribable, and I fell on my face…*

> *There I beheld the Ancient of Days, whose head was white like wool, and with him another whose countenance resembled that of a man… then I enquired of one of the angels who went with me and who showed me every secret thing about this son of man, who he was, whence he was and why he accompanied the Ancient of Days. He answered and said to me, "This is the Son of Man, to whom righteousness belongs, with whom righteousness has dwelt and who will reveal all the treasures that are concealed…"*

> *I saw the Head of Days when he seated himself on the throne of his glory. And the books of the living were opened before him.*

Revelation likewise talks of hair as white as wool and as white as snow, of flames of fire, of angels numbering ten thousand times ten thousand, of the Ancient of Days, of the dead standing before His throne and of books being opened before Him. Similar images are also used in the Old Testament Books of Ezekiel and Daniel, but **the writer of Revelation 14 seems to have borrowed from 1 Enoch a picture which, as far as I know, is not found anywhere else**.

Revelation 14:20 speaks of sinners being trampled in "*the winepress of God's wrath*" whose "*blood flowed out of the press, rising as high as the horses' bridles*". This disturbing image does not come from the Old Testament. However, it is very similar to one used in the first verse of 1 Enoch 100 (a verse **which is** contained in the Dead Sea Scrolls). It speaks of a terrible day of God's wrath when "***the horse shall walk up to its breast in the blood of sinners***".

Then, in a deeply meaningful reference to Christ and His elect, Revelation 17:14 speaks of *"the Lamb"* who is *"King of kings and Lord of lords, and with him will be his called, elect and faithful followers"*.

Now the titles *"Lord of lords"* and *"King of kings"* are never used **together** in the Old Testament. But **Chapter 9 of 1 Enoch** (another of the chapters found at Qumran) contains the statement:

> *"You are Lord of lords, God of gods, King of kings. The throne of your glory is for ever and ever"*.

The titles *"Lord of lords"* and *"King of kings"* are again used together in Revelation 19 and are famously quoted in the 'Hallelujah Chorus' from Handel's 'Messiah'. Just as Handel has taken the words of his oratorio from the Bible, it seems the writer of Revelation has (like the writer of Jude) taken some wording from the Book of 1 Enoch!

A further notable characteristic of Revelation which resembles 1 Enoch is its frequent use of the number seven.

In Judaism, the number seven represents both completeness and blessing. The Sabbath is of course the seventh day (Saturday); Jewish Law required the land to be left uncultivated every seventh year; and the Jewish *menorah*, the iconic lamp of the Temple, has seven branches (although there is also the *Chanukah menorah*, which has nine).

As we've seen, seven is especially significant in Zoroastrianism, with its belief in the seven Spirits of God. (Remarkably, the term *"the seven spirits of God"* is used in Revelation 3:1, in Revelation 4:5 and again in Revelation 5:6.) The number seven also features prominently in the Book of Daniel (which, in Chapter 9, speaks of *"seventy sevens"*) and in 1 Enoch (which, in Chapter 20, names seven archangels). These two books were popular with Essenes who, it seems to me, were rather fixated with the number seven.

Similarly, Revelation not only refers to the seven Spirits of God, but to seven churches, to seven golden lampstands, to seven stars, to seven angels, to seven seals, to seven horns, to seven eyes and to seven years of judgement. And it also speaks of seven trumpets, seven thunders, seven heads, seven crowns, seven plagues, seven bowls, seven mountains and seven kings!

In addition to the fifty or so explicit uses of the number seven in Revelation, Bible students have identified yet more 'sevens' in it. There are seven beatitudes (found in Revelation 1:3, 14:13, 16:15, 19:9, 20:6, 22:7 & 22:14) and seven references to *"the Abyss"*. And then there are seven divisions to each of the letters to the seven churches in Chapters 2 & 3 and seven attributes of *"the Lamb"* described in Chapter 5.

So, as well as clear links between the Book of 1 Enoch and the Letters of Jude and 2 Peter, there are therefore some striking similarities between 1 Enoch and the Book of Revelation.

34. 'SON OF MAN'

Another compelling feature of the Book 1 Enoch is its repeated use of the title "*the Son of Man*" (although, admittedly, not used in any of the chapters which have been found at Qumran). The title is, of course, one which was frequently used by Jesus. **I have often wondered – as countless other Christians have no doubt done – why Jesus chose this particular title for Himself and why no one is recorded in the Gospels as having asked Him what it meant.**

The term *"son of man"* – the Hebrew word *'ben-adam'* – occurs over one hundred times in the Old Testament. Most of these are in the Book of Ezekiel, where it is used by or on behalf of God to refer to the prophet Ezekiel himself. However, **the word *ben-adam* is not a title**. As I understand it, *ben-adam* is simply another term for a human being and is used to emphasise the **weakness** of man compared to the awesome power of Almighty God.

In contrast to the use of the term *"son of man"* in Ezekiel (where it underlines human weakness), Chapter 7 of the Book of Daniel recounts the vision of "one ***like a*** *son of man, coming with the clouds of heaven*" who "*was given authority, glory and sovereign power*". Verse 14 says he was worshipped by people of every language and continues, *"His dominion is an everlasting dominion that will not pass away, and his kingdom is one that will never be destroyed".*

Many Old Testament scholars believe the Book of Daniel was written by various authors at different times, some parts of it being in the Aramaic language and other parts in Hebrew. The word in Daniel which is translated as "*a son of man*" is, I gather, an Aramaic one, *bar-enos*. Once again, this word is not a title and is usually translated simply as "*human*". Daniel 7 is therefore describing one who comes with the clouds, who receives authority, glory and power, and who has the appearance of a man.

Whilst Jesus is recorded in the New Testament as frequently using the title "*the Son of Man*", it is rarely used by others. Some Christians think He employed the title (in a similar way to which the term *"son of man"* is used in Ezekiel) to emphasise **His humanity** and in contrast to the title "*the Son of God*", which they see as asserting **His deity**.

But such an interpretation **does not** appear to fit the context of many of the verses in which Jesus is quoted as using the title *"the Son of Man"*.

On the contrary, the way it is used by Jesus is more often associated – as with the single reference to *"one like a son of man"* in Daniel 7 – with the concepts of **authority, glory and power**.

In Matthew 19:28, for example, He tells His twelve disciples:

> *"**When the Son of Man sits on his glorious throne, you who have followed me will also sit on twelve thrones judging the twelve tribes of Israel**."*

(This important quotation of Jesus presumably explains why He chose **twelve** disciples. You may recall, by the way, that the Qumran Essenes similarly had twelve of the members on their governing Council, the number also being linked in some way to the judging, or governing, of the twelve tribes of Israel.)

It is most intriguing that Jesus referred to Himself *"the Son of Man"* when the term is not used as a title in the Old Testament yet is used as a title in 1 Enoch.

Indeed, the **way** in which it was used by Him is not unlike the way it is employed in 1 Enoch. Take, for example, the following passage found in 1 Enoch 62:

> *Pain shall seize them when **they see the Son of Man sitting on the throne of his glory**; and the kings and the mighty and all who possess the earth shall bless and glorify and extol him who rules*

> *over all, who was hidden, for from the beginning the Son of Man existed in secret.*
>
> *The Most High preserved him in the presence of his might **and revealed him to the Elect**; and the congregation of the Elect and the holy shall be shown; and all the Elect shall stand before him on that day; and all the kings and the mighty and the exalted and those who rule the earth shall fall down before him on their faces and worship and set their hope upon the Son of Man.*

In much the same way, Jesus is recorded in Matthew 25:31 as declaring, *"When the Son of Man comes in His glory, and all his angels with him, **he will sit on his glorious throne**"*.

He is also quoted in Luke 17:30 as speaking of the day *"when the Son of Man is **revealed**"* and, in Luke 18:7, as asking, *"Will not God bring about justice for **his elect**... when the Son of Man comes, will he find faith on the earth?"*.

Chapters 48-51 of 1 Enoch claim that the Son of Man was named before Creation and was later revealed to *"the Elect"*:

> *Before the sun and signs were created, before the stars of heaven were made, his name was named before the Lord of Spirits.* (1 Enoch 48.3-4)

Similarly, 1 Peter 1:20 says of Christ, *"**He was chosen before the creation of the world but was revealed in these last times**"*.

1 Enoch 49 speaks of the Son of Man as the *"elect one"* or *"chosen one"*. Meanwhile, according to Luke 9:35, a voice heard during Jesus' Transfiguration declared, *"This is my son, my chosen one, listen to him"*.

However, Chapters 48-51 and Chapter 62 of 1 Enoch are all in the most recent part, the section known as *'the Book of Parables'*. This section **is not** contained in any of the copies of 1 Enoch found among the Dead Sea

Scrolls and there is no consensus among scholars as to when it was written.

Many scholars think *'the Book of Parables'* was written in around 100BC, but others believe it could have been as late as 150AD. **It is therefore possible that the chapters of 1 Enoch which refer to** *"the Son of Man"* **were not in fact written until after Jesus' ministry**.

Whilst Jesus is often quoted as referring to Himself both as *"the Son of Man"* and as *"the Son"*, He is not recorded as ever using the title *"**the Son of God**"*. It is instead a title which was attributed to Him **by others**.

The Apostle Peter, for example, is famously quoted in Matthew 16:16 as declaring: *"You are the Messiah, the Son of the living God"*. And Matthew 27:54 records that a Roman centurion at Jesus' crucifixion exclaimed, *"Surely he was the Son of God!"* (Admittedly, Luke 23:47 merely claims the centurion said, *"Surely this was a righteous man"*.)

As we've seen, the title *"the Son of Man"* **might perhaps have come from the Book of 1 Enoch. But from where, then, did the title** *"the Son of God"* **originate?**

35. 'SON OF GOD'

The Essenes saw themselves as sons, and God as their Father. In the Qumran Scrolls (in Thanksgiving Hymns 17) God is indeed addressed as *"the father of all the children of your truth"*. The Old Testament, too, contains verses in which God is likened to a father – and even some (such as Isaiah 66:13) where God is likened to a mother.

But the term *"son of God"* seldom occurs in the Old Testament and, as with the term *"son of man"*, it is never used as a title.

What is more, when the terms *"son of God"* and *"sons of God"* are used in the Old Testament, they have **no consistent meaning**, being variously used to refer to:

> (a) those (whoever they were) said in Genesis 6 to have taken wives from *"the daughters of humans"* and who, as we've previously seen, 1 Enoch claims were angels,
>
> (b) angels (presumably) once again in Job 1:6 & 2:1,
>
> (c) the mysterious fourth man described as appearing along with Shadrach, Meshach and Abednego in the *"fiery furnace"* in the story told in Daniel 3,
>
> (d) the entire nation of Israel in Hosea 1:10,
>
> (e) the heir of King David in 2 Samuel 7:14,
>
> (f) King David himself in Psalm 2:7, and
>
> (g) human rulers in Psalm 82:6.

Yet although not frequently or consistently used in the Old Testament – where it isn't a title – the term *"Son of God"* is of course one which is used as a title in the New Testament. According to Matthew 16, when Jesus asked His disciples, *"Who do you say I am?"*, Simon Peter replied: *"You are the Messiah, the Son of the living God"*. In recording Peter's reply, Mark 8 (for whatever reason) fails to include the crucial words *"the Son of the living God"*. But Mark 14 says that, on the occasion when Jesus walked to them on the water, His disciples exclaimed: *"Truly, you are the Son of God!"*

Like the Essenes, Jesus is quoted as referring to God as "*Father*" and as encouraging others to do the same. This may possibly refer to the brotherhood of **all** men, the descendants of Adam – *"the son of God"*, as Adam is described in Luke 3:38. However, the way in which the title *"the Son of God"* was employed by Jesus' followers would clearly imply they saw it as denoting **a great deal more** than simply referring to the brotherhood of mankind. It instead appears to have been a title they used to refer to something **unique** about Him, a title they connected with **the Messiah**.

Why, then, did the followers of Jesus use the title *"the Son of God"* when the term is so seldom found in the Old Testament, where it isn't a title? And why did they use it along with the title *"the Messiah"* when no such a connection is at all obvious? For centuries Christians have thought this must be something that can **only** have been revealed to them directly by God Himself.

36. QUMRAN FRAGMENTS 4Q246 AND 4Q521

Apart perhaps from a common link to King David, there is no clear interconnection in the Old Testament between the term *"son of God"* and person of the Messiah. It had therefore always appeared that the belief in Jesus as both *"the Messiah"* **and** *"the Son of God"* could not be explained within the context of the existing theologies held by Jewish people at the time of Jesus.

However, some staggering discoveries among the Dead Sea Scrolls have shed significant new light on this issue, revolutionising understanding of Jewish beliefs in the late Second Temple Period.

One Fragment, which appears to contain references to the Messiah and is known as **4Q246** (document number 246 from Qumran Cave 4) makes the following astonishing statements:

> **He shall be called the Son of God. They will call him Son of the Most High... His kingdom is an everlasting kingdom, and all his ways are truth. He will judge the earth with truth, and all will make peace.**

This enlightening Fragment indicates that, at the time of Jesus, there were indeed those who believed the Messiah would have the title *"the Son of God"*, that he would judge the earth and his kingdom would be an eternal one of truth and peace.

Some scholars do not think the above statements in 4Q246 were intended by the writer to refer to the Messiah. Yet the wording shares unmistakable similarities with several New Testament passages referring to Christ.

The most obvious is Luke 1:32-35, which famously records that the angel Gabriel, foretelling the birth of Jesus, told the Virgin Mary:

> *"He will be great and **will be called the Son of the Most High**. The Lord God will give him the throne of his father David, and he will reign over Jacob's descendants for ever. **His kingdom will never end**... The Holy Spirit will come on you and the power of the Most High will overshadow you. So the holy one to be born **will be called the Son of God**."*

The similarities between these verses in Luke 1 and the wording found in 4Q246, as quoted above, are truly striking.

Then, as regards the statement in 4Q246 *"He will judge the earth with truth"*, John 5 quotes Jesus as saying, *"The Father judges no one but has entrusted all judgement to the Son"* (verse 22) and *"He has given him authority to judge because he is the Son of Man"* (verse 27).

Unfortunately, the whole of the scroll from which Fragment 4Q246 comes hasn't survived and its full message is not known. But the portion we do have allows us to see such Bible passages in an entirely new light and to better understand Jewish expectations at the time of Jesus. **It would now appear that Essenes awaited a coming Messiah who would judge the earth, whose kingdom would never end, and who would be given the titles "the Son of God" and "Son of the Most High"**.

Another amazing Qumran Fragment, only published in 1992, is **4Q521**. Drawing on phrases used in various parts of the Book of Isaiah, it prophesies the following regarding the Messiah:

> *He will release the captives, **make the blind see** and raise up the downtrodden. For ever I will cleave to him against the powerful and I will trust in his loving-kindness and in his goodness for ever. His holy Messiah will not be slow in coming and, as for the wonders that are not the work of the Lord, **when he that is the Messiah comes then he will heal the sick, resurrect the dead and to the poor announce glad tidings. He will lead the holy ones; he will shepherd them**.*

It is astounding to think these words were written prior to Jesus' birth and were probably being read by Essenes during His life on earth!

Once again, this Qumran document has striking similarities to several verses in the New Testament. In John 10, for example, Jesus is famously quoted as teaching, "[the shepherd] *calls his own sheep by name* **and leads them out**... **I am the good shepherd**".

A further example is found in Matthew 11:

> *When John [the Baptist] heard in prison what Christ was doing he sent his disciples to ask him, "Are you the one who has come, or should we expect someone else?" Jesus replied, "Go back and report to John what you hear and see.* **The blind receive sight***, the lame walk, those who have leprosy are cured, the deaf hear,* **the dead are raised***, and the good news is preached to the poor."*

Jesus' reply to John's disciples is reminiscent of the following words He is recorded (in Luke 4:18) as having, on another occasion, read from the scroll of Isaiah handed to Him in the synagogue in Nazareth:

> *"The Spirit of the Lord is on me, because he has anointed me to proclaim good news to the poor. He has sent me to proclaim freedom for the prisoners and recovery of sight for the blind, to set the oppressed free, to proclaim the year of the Lord's favour."*

This reading is taken from Isaiah 61:1, but the words are not the same as those found in our Old Testament. The scroll of Isaiah from which Jesus read seemingly contained different wording. **Unlike the version of Isaiah in our Bibles, it talks (as Fragment 4Q521 also does) of the blind receiving sight**.

In addition, no reference is made – **either** in the version of Isaiah 61:1 quoted in Luke 4:18 **or** in the one in our Old Testament – to the dead being raised (as in the words of Jesus in Matthew 11:5 quoted above). **But astonishingly, 4Q521 does refer to the Messiah raising the dead.**

I therefore wonder if both Jesus and John the Baptist were familiar with the prophecy contained in 4Q521 and if Jesus referred to it in order to convince John He was the Messiah.

It is not possible to know with any certainty if this was the case. Neither, of course, can we know what else was written during the Second Temple Period and has not survived or has yet to be discovered. But Qumran Fragments 4Q246 and 4Q521 provide a revealing insight into the likely expectations of the Essenes regarding the role of the Messiah.

Astoundingly, Essenes seem to have believed that the Messiah would not only be called "*the Son of God*" but would also heal the sick, would give sight to the blind and would even raise the dead.

37. 'WORKS OF THE LAW' AND 4QMMT

Six of the fragments found in Qumran Cave 4 (4Q394, 4Q395, 4Q396, 4Q397, 4Q398 & 4Q399) appear to be from one document, known by scholars as 'the Halakhic Letter', or as '4QMMT'.

It is believed by leading experts on the Qumran Scrolls (such as Professor Martin Abegg, a Director of the Dead Sea Scrolls Institute) to be a copy of an important letter written to the Jewish leaders in Jerusalem by the Essenes in the early years of the group's existence.

The fragments are incomplete, but the Letter is in three sections.

The first section refers to the Calendar with a 364-day year, which was used by the Essenes and which we looked at in Chapter 27.

The second part of the Letter sets out 22 detailed regulations, favoured by the Essenes, relating (amongst other things) to the way in which sacrifices should be conducted.

Interestingly, the 22 regulations are collectively referred to in 4QMMT as "**works of the law**", a term which is not used in the Old Testament nor (to the best of my knowledge) in **any other** pre-Christian literature.

However, although not found in the Old Testament, this Qumran term is one which is employed by the Apostle Paul.

The phrase *"works of the law"* is used both in Romans 3 and in Paul's letter to the churches of Galatia. In Galatians 2:16, for example, he says:

> "...a person is not justified by the **works of the law**, but by faith in Jesus Christ. So, we too have put our faith in Christ Jesus, that we may be justified by faith in Christ and not by the **works of the law**, because by the **works of the law** no one will be justified".

4QMMT uses the term *"works of the law"* to refer to the observance of specific rules and regulations, and not to mean good works in the general sense.

Essenes seemingly held that a person is justified as a result of being repentant **in heart** and not merely by observing religious rituals – crucial though they clearly believed each small detail (every 'jot and tittle') of the rules relating to those rituals to be. Jesus likewise emphasised the vital importance of what is in your heart. And, at the same time, He is recorded (in Matthew 5:17-20) as saying He had not come to abolish **even the tiniest detail** of Jewish Law, but to **fulfil** it, concluding:

> *"...unless your righteousness **surpasses** that of the Pharisees and the teachers of the law, you will certainly not enter the kingdom of heaven."*

The third and final part of 4QMMT is an entreaty to the Jewish leaders in Jerusalem to adopt the Essene Calendar and the 22 additional regulations (or *"works of the law"*) which the Essenes advocated. This appeal was evidently rejected, leaving the Essenes using a different calendar and having some different religious practices from the rest of Jewish society.

38. SECRETS AND ASCENSIONS

Another passage written by Paul with similarities to some of the Dead Sea Scrolls can be found in 2 Corinthians 12:2-4, where he makes the following astonishing claim:

> *I know a man in Christ who 14 years ago **was caught up to the third heaven**. Whether it was in the body or out of the body I know not – God knows. And I know that this man, whether in the body or apart from the body I do not know but God knows, **was caught up to paradise and heard inexpressible things, things that no one is permitted to tell**.*

Understandably, there has been a good deal of discussion among Christians as to how these unusual verses in 2 Corinthians should be interpreted. It is widely agreed, however, that *"this man"* to whom Paul refers is most likely the Apostle himself.

The term "*third heaven*" does not occur anywhere else in the Bible and, surprisingly, Paul offers no guidance as to its meaning, appearing to assume his readers are familiar with it. He also calls it ***"paradise"***. The name paradise (you will no doubt recall) was used by Josephus to refer to the beautiful place refreshed by gentle breezes, to which Essenes believed the souls of the righteous go immediately after death. And in Luke 23:43, the name is recorded as having been used by Jesus, when He said to the dying criminal on the cross beside Him, *"Truly I tell you, today you shall be with me in paradise"*.

In 2 Corinthians 12, Paul says he does not know if the man's ascension to the third heaven was a physical one or was instead some sort of out-of-body experience. Either way, his record of a man being caught up to paradise is quite extraordinary. (As mentioned earlier, the Book of 1 Enoch and the Letter to the Hebrews each make a similar claim about none other than the Old Testament character **Enoch**.)

Remarkably, others of the Qumran Scrolls also relate stories of people ascending to heaven during mystical religious experiences. These accounts of ascensions in the Scrolls, I gather, are much like that described by Paul in 2 Corinthians 12.

Qumran Fragments 4Q491 & 4Q427, for example, describe an ascension to heaven by a man thought by Professor Martin Abegg to have been the so-called *"Teacher of Righteousness"*, the one-time leader of the Essene movement. (See *'Who Ascended to Heaven? 4Q491, 4Q427 and the Teacher of Righteousness'* by M.G. Abegg.)

Some have suggested these experiences were induced by hallucinogenic plants or roots. But – apart perhaps from the passing reference made by Josephus to Essenes using various plants and roots – there is very little evidence to support the theory.

The mystical ascensions described in the Scrolls were seemingly reserved for a select number of people. And they were linked to the discovery of mysteries which, as with the *"inexpressible things"* heard during the ascension described by Paul, no one was permitted to tell.

They also share some interesting similarities with the Gospel accounts of the extraordinary event in the life of Jesus known as the Transfiguration.

Matthew 17, Mark 9 & Luke 9 each tell of an occasion when Jesus took the disciples Peter, James and John and ascended an unnamed mountain, where He was *"transfigured"*. As Jesus was praying, His appearance changed, His clothes became a dazzling white, and two men – Moses and Elijah – appeared and spoke with Him.

Several aspects of the Gospel accounts of this ascension are mysterious. None of them explain, for example, **how** the three disciples identified the men as Moses and Elijah. And, despite the astonishing events unfolding before them, Luke says that Peter and his companions became very **sleepy**, awakening from their slumber to see Jesus' **glory**.

As happened to Jesus (according to Acts 1) during His Ascension, Luke says they then entered a **cloud**. From the cloud came a **voice** that declared, "*This is my Son, whom I have chosen; listen to him*".

The Gospels do not explain why Jesus selected only Peter, James and John for this mystical experience. According to Mark 5:37, they were the only people Jesus allowed to go along with Him when He raised to life the daughter of the synagogue official Jairus. And it was the same three who, as recorded in Mark 14:33, He took aside with Him to pray in the Garden of Gethsemane on the night of His arrest.

It would therefore seem that Jesus took these three disciples into His confidence in a way He didn't do the others. Indeed, Matthew 17:9 says **He instructed them to tell no one** (presumably including the rest of the disciples) of what they had seen until after the Resurrection.

Once again, no reason is given in the Gospels for Jesus' instruction not to tell anyone. It is reminiscent (is it not?) of both the oath Josephus claims was made by Essenes to keep certain things secret and the instruction in the Qumran Community Rule that the "***secrets of knowledge***" should be kept hidden.

It is also like the ascensions described in the Dead Sea Scrolls, where the revelation of mysteries to a select number of people could not be disclosed to others. And, of course, it has an obvious similarity with Paul's account in 2 Corinthians 12 of the ascension of a man to the third heaven, where he heard "*things that no one is permitted to tell*".

Surprisingly, the Gospel of John does not refer to the Transfiguration – other perhaps than indirectly with the words in John 1:14: "*we have seen his glory*".

Yet not only is the Apostle John recorded as being a participant in the amazing experience, but it is an express objective of John's Gospel (as outlined in John 20:31) to show "*that Jesus is the Messiah, the Son of God*".

A possible explanation for this omission could be that John **continued** to keep the Transfiguration a secret throughout his life.

(I'm aware that very few New Testament scholars today believe the fourth Gospel was actually **written** by the Apostle John. But I gather it is thought the Gospel could possibly have been written by a member of a group which was founded by John or was in some other way associated with him.)

39. JANNES, BELIAL AND MELCHIZEDEK

There are some further intriguing similarities between the New Testament and the Dead Sea Scrolls in the use of certain **names**. 2 Timothy 3:8, for example, says the following about some false teachers:

> Just as **Jannes and Jambres** opposed Moses, so also these men oppose the truth, men of depraved minds who, as far as the faith is concerned, are rejected.

The names Jannes and Jambres are not used anywhere else in the Bible, yet no explanation is given in 2 Timothy as to their identity. So, just who are they?

In Jewish tradition, I gather, Jannes and Jambres were brothers. They are said to have been among the Egyptian magicians with secret arts referred to in Exodus 7 and who, as Aaron had done, threw down staffs before Pharaoh which turned into snakes. Although not ever named in the Old Testament, Jannes and his brother **are** mentioned in the Scrolls.

Early Christian sources refer to a **Book** of Jannes and Jambres. Although we now have only a few small surviving fragments of this book, it was evidently in circulation among Christians during the first and second centuries. It did not claim to be written by Jannes or Jambres but, as I understand it, the book recounted wicked exploits of the pair, who were said to have been sons of the Old Testament character **Balaam**.

The remarkable tale of Balaam and the donkey which spoke to him is told in Numbers 22-24. Balaam's prophesies (or oracles) are related in several of the Qumran Scrolls, but the wording in each Scroll differs (see *'A Star from Jacob, a Sceptre from Israel: Balaam's Oracle as Rewritten Scripture in the Dead Sea Scrolls'* by Libor Marek).

It would therefore seem that the Balaam story was an important one for the Essenes.

Significantly, references to Balaam are also made in the New Testament, in what we may by now be tempted to call 'the usual suspects' – the Letters of Jude and 2 Peter and the Book of Revelation!

Jude (as we saw previously) condemns certain men who have rejected authority and who *"heap abuse on celestial beings"*, declaring in verse 11:

> *Woe to them! They have taken the way of Cain; they have rushed for profit into **Balaam's error**...*

2 Peter 2 likewise condemns those who *"cast abuse on celestial beings"*, stating in verses 14 & 15:

> *They have left the straight way and wandered off to follow the way of **Balaam**, son of Bezer, who loved the wages of wickedness. But he was rebuked for his wrongdoing by a donkey – an animal without speech – who spoke with a human voice and rebuked the prophet's madness.*

And Revelation 2:14 conveys the following reprimand to the Christian Church in Pergamum:

> *There are some among you who hold to the teaching of **Balaam**, who taught* [the foreign king] *Balak to entice the Israelites to sin so that they ate food sacrificed to idols and committed sexual immorality.*

In each of these passages, Christians who have gone astray and have engaged in sinful practices are likened to the prophet Balaam, who was believed to be the father of Jannes and Jambres.

As for the name Jannes, the first known reference to it in any literature is, to the best of my knowledge, in Damascus Document 5.7, which states that *"Jannes and his brother"* were raised up by *"Belial"*. The name of Belial, who the Damascus Document claims raised up Jannes and Jambres, is used in various other Qumran Scrolls. And it is also found in 2 Corinthians 6:15, which poses the rhetorical question:

*What harmony is there between Christ and **Belial**?*

Another significant name appearing in the Scrolls is that of **Melchizedek**, someone who is mentioned briefly in two places in the Old Testament. The first of these is in Genesis 14, which records that as Abram returned from a victorious battle:

> *Then Melchizedek, king of Salem, brought forth bread and wine. He was the priest of the Most High God. And he blessed him and said, "Blessed be Abram of the Most High God, Creator of heaven and earth"* (Genesis 14:18-19).

Genesis says Abram then gave Melchizedek a tenth of everything. Not much else is said about Melchizedek in the Old Testament, but the following statement is made in Psalm 110:4:

> *The Lord has sworn and shall not change His mind: "You are a priest forever in the order of Melchizedek"*.

In Hebrews 7, these words in Psalm 110 are applied to **Jesus**. The writer draws parallels between Christ and the priest/king Melchizedek, whose name means *"king of righteousness"* and whose description as king of Salem means *"king of peace"*. He declares in verse 3 that Melchizedek is:

> *without beginning of days or end of life, resembling the Son of God, he remains a priest forever.*

However, before the Letter to the Hebrews was written, the name of Melchizedek featured prominently in the Scrolls. Most notably, it is found in Qumran document 11Q13, which has come to be known as **the Melchizedek Fragment**.

Only parts of the original document have survived, and its full message is unknown, but 11Q13 evidently links Melchizedek with **the Messiah**. It associates him with the chosen one who brings the good news of atonement for the sins of *'the Sons of Light'*, and to whom is given the judgement of the world. It even appears to connect the name of Melchizedek with that of God Himself.

Interestingly, **the Fragment portrays Melchizedek as being the leader of 'The Sons of Light'** who will lead them, along with God's angels, in a glorious final victory over '*the Sons of Darkness*'.

And in it, as in various Dead Sea Scrolls, **the leader of '*the Sons of Darkness*' is named as none other than Belial** – the same name which (as we've seen) is used by Paul in 2 Corinthians 6!

To summarise then, 2 Timothy refers to Jannes and Jambres – wicked brothers who are not mentioned in the Old Testament but who the Damascus Document claims were raised up by Belial. 2 Corinthians likewise speaks of Belial – a name frequently occurring in the Scrolls, where he is said to be the leader of '*the Sons of Darkness*'. And Hebrews 7 links Jesus with Melchizedek, who Essenes believed would be leader of '*the Sons of Light*' in their ultimate victory over Belial and '*the Sons of Darkness*'.

40. FULL CIRCLE

And so, having returned to the subject of the battle between *'the Sons of Light'* and *'the Sons of Darkness'*, I seem to have come full circle.

As I sat in the Jerusalem sun all those years ago, mid-way between the white dome of *the Shrine of the Book* (representing *'the Sons of Light'*) and that black polished granite wall (symbolising *'the Sons of Darkness'*) I couldn't have imagined where my subsequent quest to learn about the Essenes would take me!

I am truly thankful for my Christian upbringing, glad to have been brought up to read the wonderful and varied collection of Jewish literature we know as the Old Testament and consequently to appreciate the Jewish foundations of Christianity. However, I had been taught there was a great silence in the years between the completion of the Protestant Old Testament and the birth of Christ. I now find that position to have been challenged beyond breaking point.

Undoubtedly, Christianity can only be fully understood within the context of the Judaism of the Old Testament, which is continuously alluded to throughout the New. But if it is to be viewed **honestly**, then surely Christianity **must also** be seen in the context of Judaism as it had become in the late Second Temple Period.

Can we with honesty continue to ignore (as many appear to do) the relevance to Christianity of the Essene *'Sons of Light'* – who were themselves likely influenced by the beliefs of the Zoroastrians?

A striking example of this influence is the seemingly sudden introduction in the New Testament of the concept of **demons** which cause illness and must be cast out of some of those who are sick, if they are to be healed. Such a concept doesn't feature in the Old Testament. But it is evident from the record of Josephus, from the Dead Sea Scrolls and from the reference in Matthew's Gospel to others casting out demons, that this was not a new practice introduced by Jesus. Believed by the Essenes (and by at least some of the Pharisees) it had clearly **already** become a part of Second Temple Period Judaism.

And perhaps of even greater importance than the subject of demons is that of **angels**. Zoroastrian priests ("*magi*") placed considerable emphasis upon both angels and the stars, which, as we have seen, are linked together in the Bible.

The Essenes shared with the Zoroastrians this fascination with angels and archangels on the one hand and with the stars and planets on the other, possibly even believing the stars ("*the heavenly host*") **to be** angels (and thus messengers) and the sun, the moon and the planets to be the archangels.

Can it be without significance that the New Testament – in common with the books of the Essenes, but in contrast to the Old Testament – talks of archangels?

And is it merely coincidence that the Letters of Jude and 2 Peter refer to fallen angels who are kept in chains and are awaiting their judgement, something which is described in the Book of 1 Enoch but not in the Old Testament? Perhaps so.

Yet 1 Enoch played a significant part, not only in Essene theology, but also in the early Christian Church. As we've seen, the writer of Jude even **quotes** from 1 Enoch – a fact I hadn't realised before starting my research into the Essenes. Indeed, for much of my life I was completely unaware of the existence of the Book of 1 Enoch, let alone of its various connections to the Bible.

Of all I have learned from my research, the most compelling are the numerous parallels between the teachings of the New Testament and what the contents of the Qumran Scrolls, the results of archaeological excavation and the records of ancient historians like Josephus tell us about the Essenes.

So, let me recap some of the similarities and/or connections I've come across.

Before commencing his public ministry, John the Baptist is said in Luke's Gospel to have lived, as the Qumran Community did, in the wilderness of Judea. He preached not far from Qumran and baptised converts in a similar way to the Essenes.

He is recorded as having lived simply and, in Luke 3:11, as having advocated the sharing of food and clothing. Essenes likewise had a simple lifestyle, sharing their food and clothing.

Remarkably, the Gospels identify John, in exactly the same way the Qumran Community identified themselves, with the voice of one described in the Book of Isaiah, calling in the wilderness, *"Prepare the way of the Lord!"*

John's unusual diet is said to have been locusts and wild honey. The Qumran Community Rule instructed Essenes not to eat food provided by anyone other than the Community. In order to remain true to their solemn vow not to accept food from non-Essenes, Josephus says, those who were expelled had to obtain their own food from the land. For a first century Bear Grylls attempting to survive in such a way in the Judean desert, wild honey and locusts (insects which are a valuable source of protein and are mentioned as food in some of the Scrolls) would almost certainly have been on the menu!

And Essenes would undoubtedly have regarded the marriage of Herod Antipas to his brother's ex-wife Herodias – who also happened to be his niece – to be sinful. John sadly lost his life as a consequence of expressing this same view.

Even though Josephus makes no reference in his writings to any link, a connection between John the Baptist and the Essenes seems likely.

Josephus also doesn't mention there being any connection between John and Jesus. But the Gospels speak of numerous links between them, including that they were related to one another, that Jesus was baptised by John, and that they used some of the very same phrases. All the recorded teachings of John are contained in those of Jesus, including his key message of the urgent need for people to repent because (as Essenes also believed) the kingdom of God, and His judgement upon the unrighteous, was close at hand.

As Essenes would have done, John and Jesus are each recorded as strongly criticising the Sadducees and the Pharisees, but not as expressly using the name 'Essenes'.

Josephus states that, although the sect had many collective assets, Essenes despised personal possessions and shared everything together. Jesus is quoted as similarly teaching that it is impossible to serve both God and money. Indeed, the Essene attitude to personal possessions is succinctly summarised in the words of Jesus in the Sermon on the Mount: "*Do not store up **for yourselves** treasure on earth*".

It is notable that, just as the Essenes would have done, Jesus is quoted as declaring, "*Those of you who do not give up everything you have cannot be my disciples*" and as telling a man, "*Go and sell everything you have and give to the poor*". Indeed, not only did the Essenes require converts to sell all their possessions and give the proceeds to a common fund but they also regarded themselves as **being** '*the Poor*'.

Astonishingly, the first Christians are documented in the Book of Acts as having acted similarly, not treating any of their possessions as their own, selling assets, handing over the proceeds to their leaders and sharing everything they had. In this respect, they were acting in the same way as Essenes.

It must have been extremely difficult for a rich man to take the step of joining the Essenes. They would surely have discovered from experience that (in the words of Jesus in Matthew 19) "*it is easier for a camel to go through the eye of a needle than for someone who is rich to enter the kingdom of God*"!

As Jesus of course did, Essene teachers are said (by the ancient Jewish historian Philo) to have often used allegories, or parables.

And like Jesus, Essenes engaged in the practice of healing the sick. Given that some of the Qumran Scrolls identify Psalms to be recited when exorcising those who were ill, this evidently included (as with Jesus) the casting out of demons.

Jesus, like John the Baptist, preached to the Jewish public, *"the lost sheep of Israel"*. He is famously quoted in Matthew's Gospel as teaching that your *"lamp"* shouldn't be hidden *"under a bowl"* but should be placed on a stand so as to provide light for others. These words, with their strong sense of irony, would likely have been interpreted by at least some of His listeners as a criticism of those Essenes who – although claiming to be '*the Sons of Light*' and *"a voice"* crying in the wilderness – had remained closeted away at Qumran!

Some of the Essene groups living elsewhere may well have felt the Qumran Community had been remiss in not enlightening their fellow Jews, warning them of God's coming judgement upon the nation and calling upon them to repent before it was too late. Essenes who held such a view would have seen the Qumran leaders as having wasted the assets which had been entrusted to them as stewards by failing to use them to benefit others. This could possibly be the message Jesus intended to convey in the Parable of the Unjust Steward. Whilst some may regard such an interpretation as highly speculative, two factors should be borne in mind. Firstly, there would not seem to be any more clearly obvious meaning to the Parable, which has confused Christians for centuries. And secondly, Jesus is recorded as **using** in the Parable the term **"*the sons of light*"** – one which was strongly identified with the Essenes.

Another apparent criticism of the Qumran Essenes by Jesus was His instruction not to follow those who said you should *"love your neighbour and hate your enemy"*. No such saying is to be found in the Old Testament. Both the writings of Josephus and the contents of the Community Rule, however, reveal that it was the Essenes – or at least those Essenes based at Qumran – who taught members to love their brethren (*'the Sons of Light'*) and to hate their enemies (*'the Sons of Darkness'*).

Whilst on the one hand condemning the practice of hating your enemies, Jesus (in common with the Essenes) instructed His disciples to show love to each other, telling them, *"As I have loved you, you must love one another"*. And, interestingly, Josephus describes Jesus' followers as being those who had *"come to love Him"* and whose affection for Him had endured long after His death.

A further feature of the Essenes highlighted by Josephus is that they refrained from expressing anger with one another. Jesus is quoted as likewise teaching: *"anyone who is angry with a brother or sister will be subject to judgement"*.

Each Essene, Josephus claims, swore to love God, to observe justice to all men and harm no one. He regarded them as peaceable folk – although that seemingly didn't prevent them expressing 'righteous anger' towards the Temple regime in Jerusalem, which they saw as being corrupt.

Jesus similarly displayed righteous anger towards the Temple system, denouncing it as a *"den of robbers"* and forcibly clearing the traders from the Temple. And, as Essenes did, Jesus preached a message of peace. He is recorded in the Gospels as teaching that the Commandments can be summarised as being, firstly, to love God with all your heart, soul, mind and strength, and secondly, to *"love your neighbour as yourself"*.

Another vow made on joining the Essenes, according to Josephus, was to be subject to all those in authority. 1 Peter similarly contains the instruction: *"Submit yourselves, for the Lord's sake, to every human authority"*, and the Apostle Paul told Christians in Rome: *"everyone must submit himself to the governing authorities"*.

Josephus says Essenes swore not to abuse whatever authority they were given. This was similar to the Zoroastrian principle that leaders should rule in righteousness and fairness. In much the same way as both, Jesus is quoted as telling His disciples: *"You know that the rulers of the Gentiles lord it over them and their high officials exercise authority over them. Not so with you"*. Once again in the Letter of 1 Peter, Christian elders were instructed to be good shepherds of the flock, not lording it over them. And in 1 Peter 5:2, they were told not to pursue *"dishonest gain"*, whilst Josephus claims that Essenes promised to refrain from *"unlawful gain"*.

Essenes are recorded as having worn simple white clothes and as having vowed not to seek to outdo one another in dress or finery. In 1 Peter (yet again) Christian wives were told, *"Your beauty should not come from outward adornment, such as elaborate hairstyles and the wearing of gold jewellery or fine clothes"*. And in the Sermon on the Mount, Jesus is quoted as asking His listeners, *"Why do you worry about clothes? See how the flowers of the field grow... I tell you that not even Solomon in all his splendour was dressed like one of these"*, possibly referring to the common white lilies found on the Galilean hillsides.

Another of the Essene vows, according to Josephus, was never to disclose, even on threat of death, certain **secrets** to outsiders. We do not of course know what these confidences were, but they may well be related to the secrets which were disclosed during the mysterious **ascensions** described in some of the Scrolls as having been experienced by a select number of people.

In an intriguing parallel, the Apostle Paul writes mysteriously of a man hearing *"things that no one is permitted to tell"* during an ascension to *"paradise"*. And the Gospels record that, following the ascension of a mountain where Jesus was *"transfigured"*, He ordered the three selected disciples who were present not to tell anyone of their experience.

Josephus records that Essenes – in contrast to many others in Jewish society – believed it to be wrong to make frequent oaths. Jesus would appear to have aligned Himself with the Essenes on this issue, telling His followers, *"Do not swear an oath... all you need to say is simply 'yes' or 'no'"*, instructions which are repeated in the Letter of James.

A further distinct feature of the Essenes, noted by Josephus and others, was their very different attitude towards **marriage**.

Quite a few of the Essenes, Josephus says, chose to remain celibate. Jesus is recorded in the Gospels not only as having Himself been unmarried but as speaking approvingly of those who had *"renounced marriage because of the kingdom of heaven"*.

According to Matthew, Jesus then went on to teach – just as the Essenes did – *"The one who can accept this **should** accept it"*. This teaching is echoed by the Apostle Paul in 1 Corinthians 7, when he encouraged single and widowed believers in Corinth to remain unmarried. (Surprisingly perhaps, the stance taken by the Essenes, by Jesus and by Paul regarding celibacy differed not only from that of most other Jews but also from the teachings of the Zoroastrians, who considered it to be a man's duty to God to marry and have children.)

As for the identity of those to whom Jesus was referring as having renounced marriage, the Essene *'Sons of Light'* who had chosen to adopt a life of celibacy are the most obvious candidates. In fact, as far as I know, they were the **only** group who would have qualified.

Several sources record that Essenes were opposed to men divorcing their wives – even though Jewish Law contained provisions which allowed them to do so. Yet again, Jesus is recorded as having taken the same minority position as the Essenes. And, although Paul (for whatever reason) seldom quotes Jesus in any of his letters, he likewise told the Church in Corinth: *"...a husband must not divorce his wife..."* Paul goes on to make clear this was not merely his own instruction but was a command of *"the Lord"*.

When Essenes travelled to another town in which there was an Essene community, Josephus says, they were provided there with all they needed and so didn't need to take anything with them on their journey, apart from a staff for personal protection. (In recording this detail, he evidently saw the practice as being peculiar to the Essenes, who shared their food and clothing.)

Astoundingly, Jesus is quoted in Mark's Gospel as having similarly instructed the twelve disciples He sent out into the countryside to preach: *"Take nothing for the journey except a staff – no bread, no bag, no money in your belts. Wear sandals but not an extra shirt"*. Perhaps the disciples were being accommodated by Essenes living in different locations around the country who – at that stage at least – were sympathetic towards Jesus' message and provided His disciples with a bed, with food and with clean clothing.

Another practice of the Essenes highlighted by Josephus is that they rose before daybreak and sought out lonely places in which they would pray. In precisely the same manner, according to Mark, *"very early in the morning, while it was still dark, Jesus got up, left the house and went off to a solitary place where He prayed"*.

At the time of Jesus, Roman coins were not accepted for the purpose of buying animals for sacrifice inside the Temple. Containing less silver than Tyrian shekels and featuring graven images of the heads of the Caesars (who were regarded as gods), the coins were seen by some Jews as 'unlawful'. At least some Essenes seemingly went so far as to refuse to use Roman currency at all, except – it must be assumed – to pay their poll-tax to the Romans.

Becoming aware of this fact has revolutionised my understanding of the passage in Mathew 22, where Jesus was asked whether or not it was right to pay tax to Caesar. According to Matthew, Jesus first requested one of the coins used to pay the tax. After making the point that it of course bore Caesar's **image**, He then gave His brilliant reply to the question about paying tax: *"So, give back to Caesar what is Caesar's and to God what is God's"*. Remarkably, these words succinctly summarise the position of using coins bearing the image of Caesar for the **sole** purpose of paying taxes to the Romans.

All of this may well be relevant to the Gospel accounts of the clearance by Jesus from the Temple courts of the money changers who exchanged Roman coins for Tyrian shekels thereby, in the eyes of at least some

Essenes, defiling the house of God. Jesus' actions in forcibly clearing the Temple and His words condemning the temple system as a *"den of robbers"* mirrored the intense righteous anger felt by Essenes towards what they believed to be a corrupt Temple regime.

But, whilst sharing the Essene view that the Temple system was corrupt, Jesus may possibly have disagreed with those Essenes who refused to engage in any trade. Both the Parable of the Unjust Steward and the Parable of the Talents could well have been interpreted by His listeners as being a criticism the Qumran leadership for their failure to use the Communities' wealth more wisely.

A policy of conducting no trade with outsiders would have been possible (if not necessarily wise) for the self-sufficient Community in Qumran, who evidently had their own mill to make flour and even their own pottery. But it would probably not have been feasible for those Essene groups who lived in Jerusalem or in other towns such as Nazareth.

On this question – and on other issues, such as compulsory celibacy and engaging in outreach to their fellow Jews – there was likely a difference of opinion between the exclusive Qumran Community and some of the other Essene groups who lived elsewhere. Jesus, it seems, was much closer to the stance taken by **these** Essene groups than He was to that of the Community at Qumran.

One of the teachings in the Qumran Community Rule which was very pointedly contradicted by Jesus is the instruction to exclude from the communal meal table the crippled, the lame and the blind. He is quoted as declaring that, when having a banquet, one should make a point of **inviting** the crippled, the lame and the blind (as well as the poor). Like the Essenes – and in contrast to many others in Jewish society – Jesus clearly did not consider poverty to be a curse from God. Unlike at least some of the Essenes, however, He appears to have regarded physical handicap in the same way.

The man mentioned in Luke 22, who [unusually] carried a jar of water, and who led the disciples Peter and John to the upper room where the Last Supper was to be held, could well have been an Essene. And the building believed since at least the third century to be its location is thought by some archaeologists to be situated in what was the Essene quarter of Jerusalem. It is beside a city gate they think may be the one referred to by Josephus as *"the Gate of the Essenes"*. If they are correct in their conclusions, Jesus may therefore have been celebrating the Last Supper with His disciples in an area of the city which was occupied by members of an Essene community.

If Jesus also used the Essene's Calendar, this could provide an interesting explanation for the difference between the timing of the Last Supper in John and that in the other Gospels. (Whilst the theory has its supporters, others are sceptical. They point both to the absence of any record of Jesus ever using the Essene Calendar and to the many other differences there are between the Gospel of John and those of Matthew, Mark & Luke.)

Chapter 20 of 1 Enoch – several copies of which were found at Qumran – names the seven archangels. The New Testament, in contrast to the Old, also refers to archangels.

The Book of Revelation even speaks of *"the seven angels who stand before God"*. This seems likely to be a reference to the seven archangels as, using similar wording, the Book of Tobit (one which is included not only in the Scrolls but also in the Old Testaments of the Catholic and Orthodox Churches) describes the archangel Raphael as *"one of the seven who stand before the Lord"*.

An extract from the first Chapter of 1 Enoch – another of the chapters in the Dead Sea Scrolls – is even quoted in the New Testament Letter of Jude, which claims the words to be those of Enoch (*"the seventh from Adam"*) himself. Indeed, the very term *"seventh from Adam"* is one which is used in 1 Enoch.

It is surely significant that the writer of Jude should choose to quote from 1 Enoch, indicating he, like the Essenes, considered it to be a book of value.

Jude (as well as 2 Peter) speaks of disobedient angels who have been bound in chains and are kept in darkness awaiting their judgement – something not mentioned in the Old Testament but described Chapter 10 of 1 Enoch (another of the chapters of 1 Enoch found at Qumran).

And in 1 Peter, Christ is said to have made proclamation to *"the imprisoned spirits"*. This unusual term – which has no other clearly obvious meaning – could well be another reference to the imprisoned angels who are described in 1 Enoch. It is claimed in 1 Enoch that these sinful angels will eventually be cast into the *"Abyss of Fire"*. (Although not found in the Old Testament, the word *"Abyss"* is also used in Luke's Gospel and in the Book of Revelation.)

Meanwhile, 2 Peter talks of the angels who sinned being thrown into *"Tartarus"* – a name taken from Greek mythology, which is not used elsewhere in the Bible but is (yet again) found in 1 Enoch.

Whilst the titles *"King of kings"* and *"Lord of lords"* are never used together in the Old Testament, they are used together in the Book of Revelation. But before Revelation was written, the two titles were found together in 1 Enoch where, as in Revelation, they are linked with an everlasting throne of glory.

1 Enoch (although not in any of the chapters found at Qumran) repeatedly speaks of *"the Son of Man"* – a title frequently used by Jesus. To the best of my knowledge, 1 Enoch is the **first** known document to have used the term *"the Son of Man"*, in the same way as Jesus did, as a title.

Jesus' followers proclaimed Him to be both *"the Messiah"* and *"the Son of God"*. These two titles are not directly associated in the Old Testament. But in some of the Scrolls the two titles **are** connected, indicating that Essenes did indeed believe the Messiah **would** be called *"the Son of God"*.

Qumran Fragment 4Q246 says the Messiah will not only be called *"the Son of God"* but will be a righteous judge of the world to whom all nations will bow – characteristics which are, of course, attributed to Christ in the New Testament.

And Qumran Fragment 4Q521 refers to the Messiah as a kind and loving shepherd (or, in other words, a **good** shepherd) who will raise up the down-trodden, heal the sick, give sight to the blind and resurrect the dead.

Essenes considered themselves to be *"the Elect"*, a term often used in 1 Enoch in connection with the Messiah. Jesus is quoted in Matthew and in Mark as similarly using the word *"elect"* in relation to events surrounding the end times. The term is also found in various New Testament books including in the Letter of 1 Peter, which is addressed to *"God's Elect"*.

The Book of Revelation, in both its style and its content, has a great deal in common with 1 Enoch. Indeed, one of the pictures used in Revelation is, to the best of my knowledge, one which can be found **only** in 1 Enoch and not anywhere else. It is the disturbing image (in Chapter 14) of a terrible Day of Judgement, when the blood of sinners will rise as high as the breasts of horses.

In the Letter to the Hebrews, Jesus is likened to Melchizedek, a person who is mentioned only briefly in the Old Testament, where he is described both as a priest and as a king. But interestingly, Melchizedek was a major figure in Essene theology, in which he is linked to the person of the Messiah. The War Scroll and the Melchizedek Fragment each claim that Melchizedek will, in a great final battle, lead the elect *'Sons of Light'* in their ultimate glorious victory over the wicked 'Sons of Darkness'.

Essenes at the time of Jesus seemingly believed God's terrible judgement upon the nation of Israel was imminent. Jerusalem, they held, was soon to be destroyed, many Jewish people would be slaughtered, and the corrupt Temple regime would be brought to an abrupt end.

According to Luke 19:44, as Jesus looked with compassion upon Jerusalem, He wept over the city, telling the people that their enemies:

> *"…will dash you to the ground, you and the children within your walls…"* and *"…will not leave one stone on another, because you did not recognise the time of God's coming to you"*.

And as Essenes also did, Jesus is quoted as (accurately) predicting the destruction of the Second Temple. Essenes apparently believed that, following its destruction, the Messiah would then miraculously raise up a **new** Temple, built in accordance with the specifications set out in the Temple Scroll. According to John's Gospel, Jesus similarly spoke of the Temple being raised again in three days (something which, because of the belief in His Resurrection, of course holds a very different and hugely significant meaning for Christians).

Essenes, in common with the teachings of the Pharisees and those of Jesus (but in contrast to the Saducees), believed in the existence of an immortal soul.

They held that, after death, the souls of the unrighteous will be subject to eternal punishment. Jesus is recorded in the Gospels as likewise speaking of never-ceasing punishment for the unrighteous. In a parable in Luke 16, for example, a rich man who lived in luxury and who had failed to share his food with a beggar named Lazarus, after death experienced torment in *"Hades"*. And, in Matthew 25:46, Jesus is quoted as saying that those who fail to provide aid to the hungry, the thirsty, the naked and those in prison *"will go away to eternal punishment"*.

According to Josephus, Essenes believed that the souls of the righteous ascend to *"paradise"*, which he interprets as being a place beyond the seas refreshed by gentle breezes. Jesus is recorded as likewise speaking of a future eternal life in paradise for *"the Elect"*. Josephus describes the Essene belief in the soul's ascent to paradise as happening immediately following death. The same expectation is expressed in the words of Jesus to a criminal being crucified beside Him: "***Today** you shall be with me in paradise*".

As the Apostle Paul did, Essenes taught that the glory of a future incorruptible life in paradise is far better than the present mortal life on this sinful earth. Consequently, they believed that (as Paul succinctly puts it in his Letter to the Philippians) "*to die is gain*".

In addition to and separate from the belief in the existence of an immortal soul (which was thought by Pharisees to remain after death in the depths of the earth, but which Essenes held would immediately rise to paradise) was a belief in a future resurrection. On 'the Last Day', the Pharisees held, the bodies of righteous Jews will be resurrected and become immortal.

According to the historian Hippolytus, the same expectation of a future bodily resurrection was shared by the Essenes. And, interestingly, archaeological investigation at Qumran reveals that many Essenes were buried in individual graves which were aligned to face in a north-south orientation. It would seem likely that this practice anticipated a future resurrection of the body.

Essenes appear to have believed that, on the Day of resurrection, '*the Elect*' (led by Melchizedek) will join God's angels (led by the archangel Michael) in a glorious victory over '*the Sons of Darkness*'.

In Matthew 24:30 Jesus is quoted as saying:

> "*...all the peoples of the earth will mourn when they see **the Son of Man** coming on the clouds of heaven, with power and great glory. And he will send **his angels** with a loud trumpet call and they will gather **his elect** from the four winds...*"

And 1 Thessalonians 4:16 declares:

> *For the Lord himself shall come down from heaven with a loud command, with the voice of the **archangel** and with the trumpet call of God, and the dead in Christ will **rise** first. After that, **we***

> ***who are still alive*** *and are left will be caught up together with them in the clouds.*

Not only did the teachings and practices of early Christians have some striking similarities with those of the Essenes, but their expectation was of the imminent return of Christ and the coming of the kingdom of God.

They believed that, heralded by an archangel, He would come down from heaven, and the bodies of those of "*his elect*" who had died would then be raised. Their expectations in this regard were not dissimilar to those of the Essene '*Sons of Light*'.

So, what conclusions can we reach?

Many people have concluded that John the Baptist was an Essene. It is perhaps more likely he was a **former** member of the Qumran Community – albeit one who had not abandoned all his Essene beliefs.

Some (like the TV presenter I mentioned in Chapter 1) claim that **Jesus** must also have been an Essene, often citing the similarities in teaching but ignoring the differences.

Others, meanwhile, disregarding the very many parallels, assert that Jesus **cannot** have been an Essene because of His public outreach, His contradiction of some of the instructions in the Community Rule and the fact He appears to have challenged an extremely strict approach to Sabbath observance.

But if Jesus had simply disagreed with the position taken by **the whole** of the Essene denomination on certain issues, **why then**, we might ask, is He not recorded in the Gospels as criticising them **by name** in the same way He so frequently did both the Pharisees and the Sadducees?

Jesus' outreach to the Jewish people contrasted with the practice of the **Qumran** Essenes, who had largely cut themselves off from the rest of society.

But it is likely some of the many **other** Essene groups, who lived elsewhere, were not as exclusive as the Qumran Community and felt they were 'hiding their light under a bushel'. This could perhaps explain why some Essenes may have provided hospitality to the twelve disciples Jesus sent out into the countryside to preach, without taking with them any money, food, or extra clothes.

As for the question of Sabbath observance, we need to bear in mind that we don't know what position was taken by each of the different Essene groups about such matters as **healing** people on the Sabbath.

Admittedly though, in rejecting an extremely strict approach to Sabbath observance Jesus seems to have – at least partly – challenged a doctrinal stance which, by all accounts, was one of those **most** associated with the Essene denomination.

Focusing on religious labels, however, can be misleading, and I am reminded of my upbringing in the Plymouth Brethren. As I have researched the Essenes, who regarded themselves as brothers, I've oft-times thought of the Brethren movement.

The term Plymouth Brethren, as with the name Essenes, is one which is generally used by others and not by members themselves. And, like the Essenes, there are within the Brethren movement various divisions, the most obvious example being those who have split away to form their own exclusive cult. Members of this cult have nothing at all to do with other Brethren groups (let alone any other churches) and, as at least some Essenes did, refuse even to **eat** with anyone who isn't a member of their own sect.

Within the 'Open Brethren' (those who are not part of the separate and exclusive cult) different local churches, known as 'assemblies', have varying positions on a range of doctrinal and practical issues. In my experience, general conversation and preaching in Brethren assemblies often centres not only upon commonly held doctrines **but also** upon those issues which **divide** them.

A central Brethren doctrine is the fundamental Protestant principle (based on 1 Peter 2:9) of 'the priesthood of all believers'. A strict application of this doctrine has led to them not having a clergy. Services in Brethren assemblies are taken either by the male members of the congregation themselves or by guest speakers.

Another commonly held doctrine (based on 1 Corinthians 14:34) is that women should not be permitted to take verbal part in church meetings. Second only to the absence of clergy, a strict adherence to the silence of women was, in my experience, one of the **most** notable features of Brethren churches. Perhaps the most eminent scholar to have belonged to a Brethren assembly was Professor F.F. Bruce, a man whose formidable intellect was exceeded only by a gracious humility. Yet Professor Bruce didn't agree with a ban on women speaking. Taking a contrary view, he cites the central principle of the priesthood of **all** believers – both men **and** women (see *'Women in the Church: A Biblical Survey'* by F.F. Bruce.) This fundamental principle, he suggests, overrides a legalistic application of Paul's practical instructions to the first century Church in Corinth.

The position taken by Jesus in relation to the Sabbath was, it appears to me, to similarly appeal to higher principles (such as the purpose for which the Sabbath had been established by God, namely for the good of man) over a legalistic interpretation of instructions.

Like Jesus, Essenes placed emphasis not just upon righteous actions but also, as Zoroastrians did, upon the mouth (in other words, upon what you say – such as swearing oaths or expressing anger with your brothers) and, above all, upon what is in your mind or "heart". For Essenes, as for Christians, the question of **purity of heart** was one of paramount importance.

First century Judaism was fragmented in a manner not entirely dissimilar to that in which Christianity is fragmented today. Attempting to define the precise differences in theology between the different groups in such an environment undoubtedly presents difficulties.

Simply because Jesus contradicted some commonly held Essene beliefs doesn't of course mean He could not have belonged to an Essene group. But hailing from Nazareth in Galilee and pointedly contradicting the Community Rule on certain issues, He was clearly **not** a member of the **Qumran** Community of Essenes. And, whilst Jesus shared some Essene practices (such as remaining unmarried and rising before dawn to pray), He evidently did not observe them **all**. He would, for example, appear to have accepted food from non-Essenes and to have dined with Pharisees as well as with the disabled and with those regarded as sinners.

Yet the views held by Essenes on various issues – views which differed from those of both Sadducees and Pharisees – are reflected time and again in the teachings of Jesus outlined in the Gospels. And, crucially, there are no doctrinal issues (of which I am aware) on which Jesus is recorded as taking the same position as that held by either the Sadducees or the Pharisees but with which the Essenes are known to have disagreed.

Much has (quite rightly) been written over many years on the centrality to Christianity of Old Testament Judaism. However, the significance of the Essenes and their teachings about such subjects as riches, sharing, oaths, anger, purity of heart, divorce, election, the kingdom of God, demons, eternal punishment, archangels, paradise, ascension and the corrupt Temple system has, I fear, been all too often overlooked.

Asking, Seeking and Knocking

In the Sermon on the Mount, Jesus is quoted as teaching:

> *"Ask and it will be given to you; seek and you will find; knock and the door will be opened to you. For everyone who asks receives; the one who seeks finds; and to the one who knocks, the door will be opened."* (Matthew 7:7)

The theme of seeking and finding is one which was often employed by Jesus. It was also a central one for Essenes, who saw themselves as *"those who seek"*. (Indeed, the Community Rule opens with the words, *"The order of the Community, **to seek God**..."* And Community Rule 8.11 says regarding new members, *"Let nothing of that which was hidden from Israel, but found by **the man who seeks**, be hidden from them"*.)

The frequent references made by Jesus to seeking are associated with His use of parables, the Hebrew word for which (*"mashal"*) can also, I understand, be translated as *"riddles"*. In a parable related in Luke 15, a woman who had lost a silver coin swept the whole house and searched diligently until she found it. And, according to Matthew 13, the kingdom of God was likened by Jesus both to the finding of buried treasure in a field and to a pearl of great value discovered by a merchant. In the same way as those joining the Essenes did, the man who found the hidden treasure sold all he had in order to buy the field and obtain the treasure. The merchant is similarly described as giving up everything he owned to secure the precious pearl.

The parable in Luke 8 of an unjust judge who granted relief to a worthy widow only because of her continued persistence in seeking justice has much in common with the parable in Luke 11 of a man who provided bread to a needy friend only because of his persistent audacity in seeking it. Although these two parables in Luke are treated by the writer as relating to prayer, the pictures of God as an unjust judge and as a lazy friend are uncomfortable, and many Bible commentators have emphasised their contrast to a just and loving heavenly Father. These parables **do**, however, reflect yet again Jesus' recurring theme of the rewards of persistence in **seeking**.

The New Testament Gospels (except for John) each record that Jesus often taught using parables. According to Matthew 13:13, He explained His use of parables as follows:

> *"This is why I speak to them in parables: Though seeing they do not see; though hearing they do not hear or understand."*

Jesus, it would appear, wanted His followers to think things through for themselves – not simply to accept what they had been told, but to ask questions, to search diligently and to seek out what is true. But the message I took from much of the instruction I received in the past (no doubt like many others from a variety of traditions, Christian and otherwise) was that unquestioning acceptance – usually but incorrectly, I think, described as faith – is positively good, whilst doubt, by the same token, is essentially bad. I no longer hold to such a view.

As I have researched the Essene *'Sons of Light'* I've been struck by information which would seem highly relevant to the contents of the New Testament, yet regarding which I was for most of my life completely in the dark. You will likely have noted, however, that from this information I have not drawn many conclusions. This has been deliberate.

Some of the conclusions I have personally come to, but which I haven't set out here, could well be incorrect. Some may change with the passage of time and with future reflection or with further discovery. At best, they are nothing more than opinions. In attempting instead to simply outline the facts I have discovered, it is my hope that it may be informative and will encourage readers to ask questions, to seek out what is truthful, to knock on a few doors and, consequently, to follow the ways of light.

© David Gaston 2023

APPENDIX

Acknowledgement

I would like to express my sincere thanks to the many friends who so kindly struggled through earlier (and even less readable) versions of this book for their helpful comments and advice, and to my darling wife Eleanor for her endless patience and support.

Sources

My main sources have been:

1. The books of the Bible, which can be read online at **BibleGateway.com** in just about any English translation you care to think of. The scripture quotations I have used are mostly taken from the Holy Bible, New International Version (Copyright 1973, 1978, 1984 & 2011 by Biblica Inc) and are used with permission, all rights being reserved worldwide.

2. The writings of the first century Jewish historian Josephus, translations of which are also freely available on several different websites, such as **Josephus.org**.

3. The Book of 1 Enoch, many copies of certain chapters of which were found at Qumran. Translations of 1 Enoch are readily available, and it is one of numerous ancient writings at **Sacred-Texts.com**.

4. The Community Rule, the Damascus Document and others of the Dead Sea Scrolls, which can be accessed online at **Deadseascrolls.org**.

5. The writings of the third century Christian writer Hippolytus, which are collectively known as *'Philosophumenia'* and are freely available at **openlibrary.org**.

6. The Book *'Every Good Man Is Free'*, by the first century historian Philo of Alexandria, which can be read at **loebclassics.com**.

7. The Book *'The Dead Sea Scrolls, A Biography'*, by John J. Collins, published by Princeton Press. Professor Collins is a renowned Yale scholar and world authority on both the Hebrew Old Testament and the Qumran Scrolls.

8. The Book *'Beyond the Qumran Community'*, also by John J. Collins, and published by William B. Eerdmans.

9. The Book *'Archaeology and the Dead Sea Scrolls'*, by Roland de Vaux, published by Oxford University Press.

10. The Book *'Second Thoughts on the Dead Sea Scrolls'*, by F.F. Bruce, published by Wipf & Stock.

Printed in Great Britain
by Amazon